# OXFORD HEROES

## 1

### Student's Book

**Jenny Quintana    Rebecca Robb Benne**

Course advisor: Norman Whitney

**OXFORD**

UNIVERSITY PRESS

# Contents

# Meet the heroes!

**1** Meet the characters.

**1** Hello, I'm Kate and this is Sam. We're eleven years old.

**2** We're friends.

**3** My name's Max. I'm the King of Crystalia. That's Imelda – she's horrible!

**4** I've got a mobile palace and a magic crystal! Ha, ha!

**5** My name's … er … oh yes, Nero. I'm a bodyguard. Imelda's my boss.

**6** Hello, I'm Tess. I'm Max's friend.

**2** Ask and answer with a partner.

Hello! What's your name?

My name's …

I'm …

**3** Make a name card.

My name's Alex

## a/an

**4** Match the pictures with the words in the box. Use *a* and *an*.

> football  cake  apple  bird  elephant
> English book  ~~ice cream~~  girl  umbrella  dog

an ice-cream

## Plurals

**5** Complete the table.

**Regular nouns**

| noun + -s | | noun + -ies | |
|---|---|---|---|
| a friend | friends | a baby | babies |
| T-shirt | 1 _____ | country | 6 _____ |
| girl | 2 _____ | story | 7 _____ |
| boy | 3 _____ | | |

| noun + -es | | noun + -ves | |
|---|---|---|---|
| a watch | watches | knife | Knives |
| bus | 4 _____ | life | 8 _____ |

**Irregular nouns**

| child | children | man | 9 _____ |
|---|---|---|---|
| woman | 5 _____ | sheep | 10 _____ |

## Numbers

**6** Match the numbers with the words in the box.

> ~~one~~  twelve  a hundred  fifteen  nine
> eighteen  four  eighty  ten  seven
> two  sixty  forty  twenty  twenty-one

| 1 one | 11 eleven | 21 _____ |
|---|---|---|
| 2 _____ | 12 _____ | 22 twenty-two |
| 3 three | 13 thirteen | 30 thirty |
| 4 _____ | 14 fourteen | 40 _____ |
| 5 five | 15 _____ | 50 fifty |
| 6 six | 16 sixteen | 60 _____ |
| 7 _____ | 17 seventeen | 70 seventy |
| 8 eight | 18 _____ | 80 _____ |
| 9 _____ | 19 nineteen | 90 ninety |
| 10 _____ | 20 _____ | 100 _____ |

**7** Play the lottery! Choose a lottery ticket and listen for your numbers.

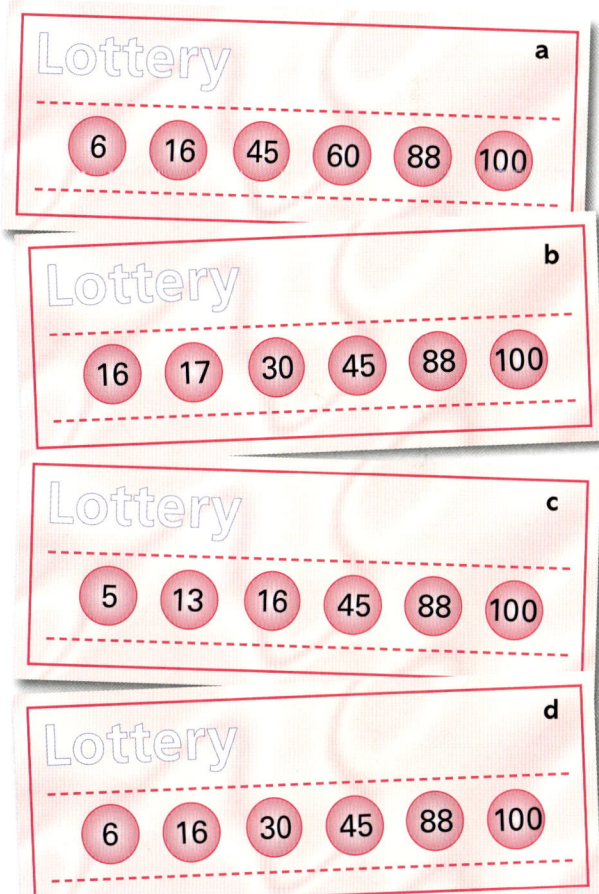

**8** Ask and answer with a partner.

> I'm ten years old. How old are you?

> I'm eleven.

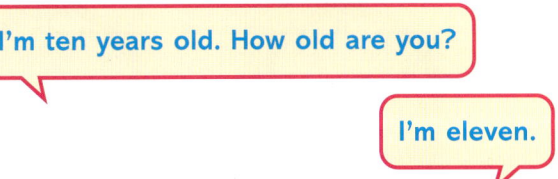

## Telling the time

**1** Listen and repeat the times. 📼

**2** Listen and choose the correct clocks. 📼

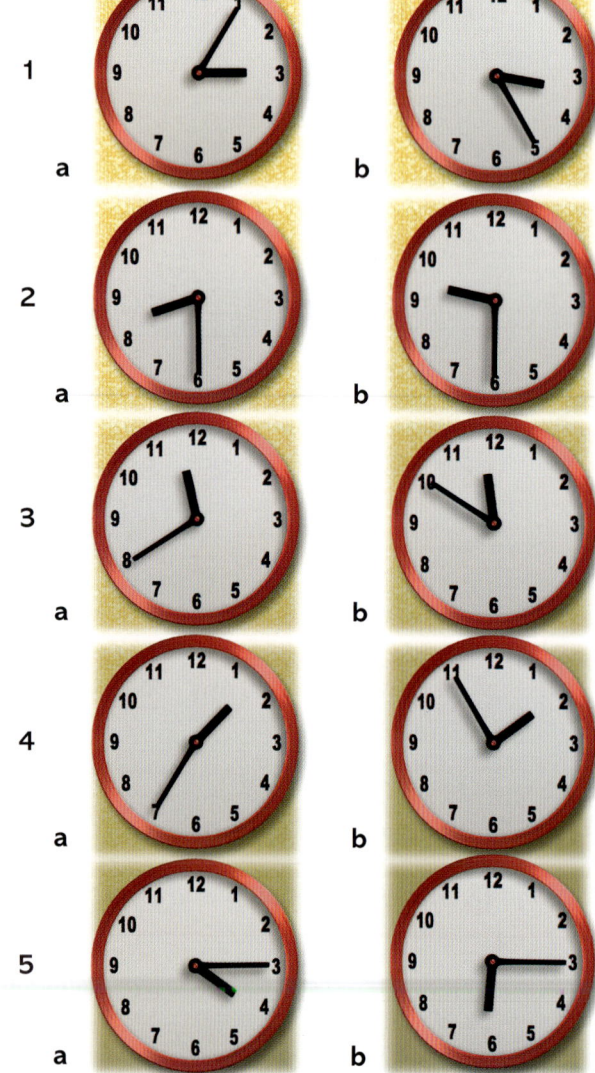

1  a    b
2  a    b
3  a    b
4  a    b
5  a    b

## Days of the week

**3** Put the days in the correct order.

### My week

Monday — 1

Friday — ☐

Wednesday — ☐

Saturday — ☐

Thursday — ☐

Tuesday — ☐

Sunday — ☐

## Months of the year

**4** Complete the months and seasons with *a, e, i, o* or *u*.

1 J_n__ry
2 F_br__ry
3 M_rch
4 _pr_l
5 M_y
6 J_n_

7 J_ly
8 __g_st
9 S_pt_mb_r
10 _ct_b_r
11 N_v_mb_r
12 D_c_mb_r

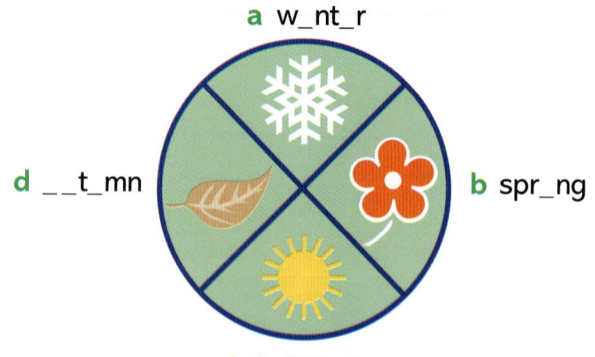

a w_nt_r

d __t_mn

b spr_ng

c s_mm_r

**5** Ask and answer about dates.

When's your birthday?

It's in November.

## Classroom language

**6** Match the pictures with the sentences in the box.

What's this in English?   Ask your partner.   Listen.
How do you spell 'friend'?   Open your books.
Look at the board.   I don't understand.   Be quiet!

①

②

③

④

⑤

⑥

⑦

⑧

## Classroom objects

**7** Match the objects in the picture with the words in the box.

desk   window   door   chair
notebook   pen   pencil   board

## Parts of the body

**8** Complete the words with *a*, *e*, *i*, *o* and *u*.

1 h _ nd
2 _ rm
3 h _ _ d
4 n _ s _
5 _ y _
6 m _ _ th
7 _ _ r
8 b _ ck
9 l _ g
10 f _ _ t

# 1 Friends

**1**  Sam and Kate are at the beach.

Sam   Catch this ball, Kate.
Kate   Wait. Who's that man?
Sam   He's strange.

**2**  They talk to Max

Max   Where am I?
Sam   You're in Britain.
Kate   I'm Kate and this is my friend, Sam.
Max   Hello. I'm Max.

**3**  Max is from a magic place.

Max   I'm the King of Crystalia.
Sam   Is that in Britain?
Max   No, it isn't. It's a magic place.
Kate   Why are you here?

**4**  Max tells his story.

Max   I've got an enemy. Her name's Imelda. She's got the magic crystal and now she's the Queen of Crystalia.
Sam   What's the magic crystal?
Max   It's my power.
Kate   We can help you.
Max   Thanks. Come with me.

**5**  Max's submarine arrives.

Max   Here's my submarine.
Sam   Wow!
Kate   Come on!

**1** Are the sentences true or false?

1  Sam and Kate are friends.
2  Max is from Britain.
3  He's a king.
4  Imelda is Max's friend.
5  The children go with Max.

**2** Find words in the story to match the pictures.

①   ② 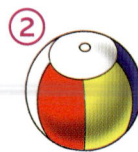  ③   ④

# Grammar

## be: present simple

| Affirmative | Negative | Interrogative |
|---|---|---|
| I am/'m | I am not/'m not | Am I ... ? |
| you are/'re | you are not/aren't | Are you ... ? |
| he<br>she is/'s<br>it | he<br>she is not/isn't<br>it | he ... ?<br>Is she ... ?<br>it ... ? |
| we<br>you are/'re<br>they | we<br>you are not/aren't<br>they | we ... ?<br>Are you ... ?<br>they ... ? |

**Short answers**
Yes, I am.    No, I'm not
Yes, she is.    No, she isn't.

**3** Complete the sentences. Use affirmative or negative forms of *be*.

1 Sam and Kate _____ eleven years old.
2 They _____ friends.
3 Max _____ on the beach.
4 Max and Tess _____ British.
5 Imelda _____ a nice person. She's horrible.
6 Max _____ the King of Crystalia.

**4** Complete the dialogue. Write the correct form of *be*.

**Tim** Hello. ¹_____ you a new student?
**Dan** Yes, I ²_____.
**Tim** ³_____ you British?
**Dan** No, I ⁴_____. I ⁵_____ from Australia. Who ⁶_____ you?
**Tim** I ⁷_____ Tim and they ⁸_____ my friends Ricky and Jake. We ⁹_____ in the school football team.
**Dan** Great. I ¹⁰_____ good at football, too.

# Listening

**5** Listen to Lily and Ben. What are their favourite sports? 🔊

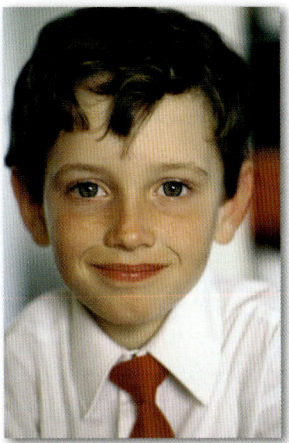

**6** Listen again. Are the sentences true or false? 🔊

1 Lily and Ben are from London.
2 They aren't classmates.
3 They're in the school music club.
4 Lily's favourite pop star is Eminem.
5 Lily is in the tennis club.
6 Ben's best friend is Lily.

# Speaking

**7** Tell the class about you and your best friends.

My name's Jack. I'm ten.

I'm Lee. My best friends are ...

My friend Jake is good at ...

# Writing

**8** Complete the sentences about you.

1 I'm at _____ School.
2 My best friend is _____.
3 My favourite pop star is _____.
4 My favourite sport is _____.
5 I'm good at _____.

# Reading

**1** Read the text. Who are Alice's best friends? 🎧

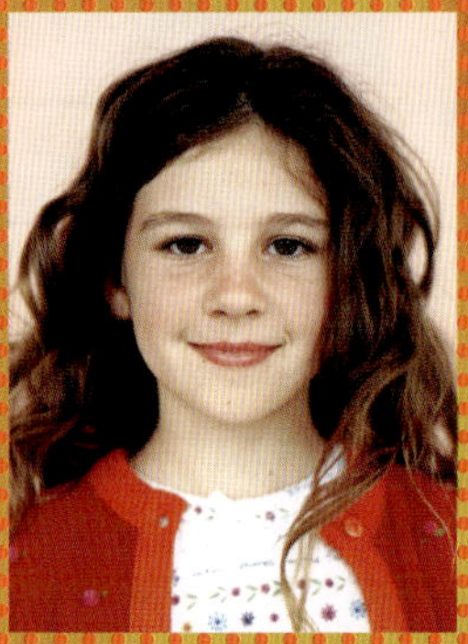

**Hello, I'm Alice.**
**Welcome to my website.**

I'm ten years old and
I'm from Edinburgh, in
5  Scotland. It's a great city.
This is Edinburgh castle.

My favourite food is pasta.
I love spaghetti!

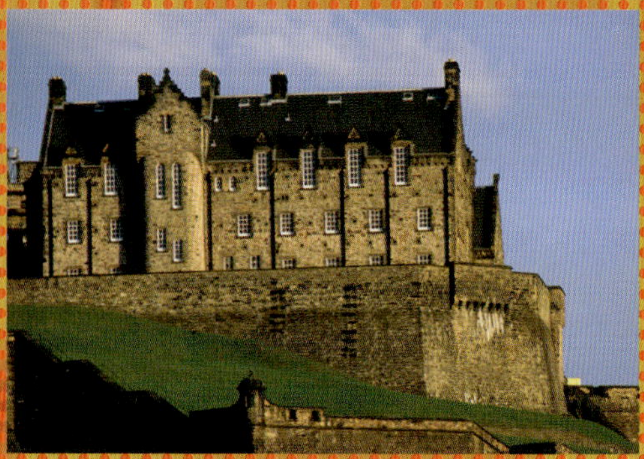

## My favourite band is
# Evanescence.
10

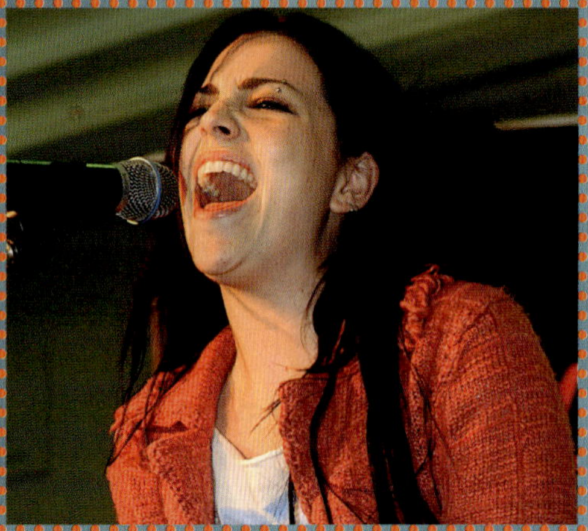

Evanescence are Amy, Ben, John and
Rocky. They're from Arkansas, in the
USA. Their music is fantastic!

**Click here for more information**

15  **My best friends**
My best friends are Maria and Kelly.
We're in a computer club together.
It's great fun! Maria is Italian, and
she's really nice. We're in the same
20  class at school. Maria's hair is black
and her eyes are brown. Kelly is my
neighbour, and she's very clever.

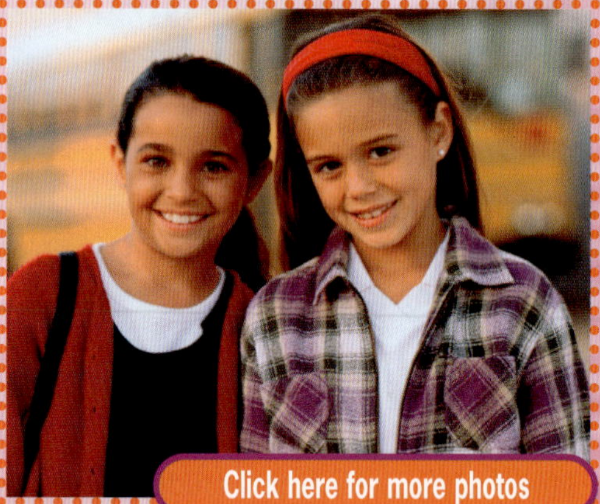

**Click here for more photos**

**Send me an e-mail! Click here.**

**2** Read the text again and answer the questions.

1  Where is Alice from?
2  What's Alice's favourite food?
3  Where are Evanescence from?
4  What club are Alice and her friends in?
5  What colour is Maria's hair?
6  Who is Alice's neighbour?

**3** Match the words from the text with the definitions.

1  great (line 5)          **a** Intelligent.
2  pasta (line 7)         **b** A person in your street.
3  band (line 9)          **c** Very nice.
4  neighbour (line 22)  **d** Italian food.
5  clever (line 22)       **e** A pop group.

**4** Do you like Alice's website? Why/Why not?.

# Grammar

## Possessive adjectives

| Personal pronouns | Possessive adjectives |
|---|---|
| I | my |
| you | your |
| he | his |
| she | her |
| it | its |
| we | our |
| you | your |
| they | their |

**5** Complete the sentences with possessive adjectives.

1 My brother is thirteen. _____ name's Tim.
2 My friend Maria is Italian. She's _____ classmate, too.
3 David and Jake are great, and _____ sister is nice, too.
4 I like _____ new website. You're very clever.
5 Simon and I are in Year 6. _____ class is 6B.

## Possessive forms

We use 's for singular nouns and names.
*the girl's bike*      *Alice's computers*
We use s' for plural nouns
*the students' desks*

**6** Write sentences with 's or s'.

Sam/desk
**It's Sam's desk.**

**1** Lucy/shoes

**2** the teachers/room

**3** Alex/clothes

**4** the girls/pet

**5** the baby/toys

# Vocabulary

## Countries and nationalities

**7** Match the flags with the countries and nationalities in the box.

France/French  Italy/Italian  Japan/Japanese
Greece/Greek  Britain/British  the USA/American

| Flag | Country | Nationality |
|---|---|---|
| | France | French |
| 1 | _____ | _____ |
| 2 | _____ | _____ |
| 3 | _____ | _____ |
| 4 | _____ | _____ |
| 5 | _____ | _____ |

# Speaking

**8** Ask and answer with a partner.

**Is he from Greece?**

**No, he isn't. He's American.**

Greece?

**1** Britain?

**2** France?

**3** Italy?

**4** Japan?

**5** USA?

## Model text

**1** Read Daniel's advert. Would you like to be his penfriend? Why/Why not?

### Kids Today Magazine

#### Penfriends section

Penfriend please!

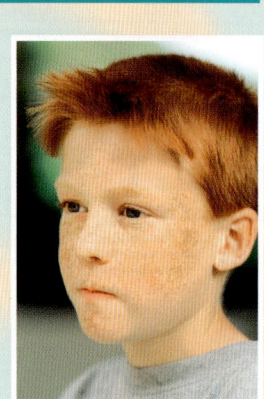

My name's Daniel and I'm British. I want a penfriend.

I'm from Oxford. It's a fantastic town! I'm eleven years old and my birthday is in February.

My favourite pop star is Robbie Williams. He's cool! I'm a good singer, too.

Are you from Turkey, Poland or Hungary? Please write to me.

**2** Read Daniel's advert again and correct the false sentences.

1 Daniel is American.
2 Oxford is a horrible town.
3 Daniel's birthday is in January.
4 His favourite pop star is Justin Timberlake.
5 He's a good footballer.

## Listening

**3** Look at the photos. Where do you think the children are from?

**4** Listen to Tiffany and Yoshio and check your answers to exercise 3. 🔊

**5** Listen again and complete the notes. 🔊

| Name | Tiffany | Yoshio |
|---|---|---|
| Nationality | 1 _____ | 5 _____ |
| City | 2 _____ | 6 _____ |
| Age | 3 _____ | 7 _____ |
| Birthday | 4 _____ | 8 _____ |

## Speaking

**6** Ask and answer with a partner.

How old are you?

Where are you from?

When's your birthday?

Who's your favourite pop star?

What's your favourite song?

# Writing

## Using capital letters

Check for capital letters in your writing.

**7** Match the rules with the examples.

We use capital letters for …

1 languages.
2 I (pronoun).
3 names of people.
4 streets and roads.
5 towns and cities.
6 days and months.
7 the first word in a sentence.
8 countries and nationalities.

a Queen Street
b Tuesday, March
c Britain, British
d Italian, Spanish
e My bike is blue.
f I'm ten.
g Sally, Mike
h London, Paris

**8** Read the postcard from Laura's penfriend. Circle the capital letters.

(S)aturday, august 10

hi laura!

i'm with my aunt in new york. new york is fantastic! my aunt's house is on canal street. it's a great street for chinese restaurants! the american people are nice, and they're very funny!

jenny

**9** Write an advert for a penfriend. Use the model text and the writing guide to help you.

Penfriend please!
My name's …
I'm from …
I'm … years old
My favourite pop star is …
Are you from …?
Please write to me.

# Song

**10** Listen and complete the song. Use the words in the box.

USA  school  door  friends  park  Greece

## My best friend

My [1] _____ are Jill, Simon and Will
And I really like Ben
We're all at [2] _____ with Ali and Paul
But you are my best friend

I live next [3] _____ to Jimmy Shaw
His sister's name is Jen
I play in the [4] _____ with Tom and Mark
But you are my best friend

My penfriend Jay's in the [5] _____
I've got a Japanese friend called Sen
My friend Kostis lives in [6] _____
But you are my best friend

SCHOOL

**11** Answer the questions.

1 Who is at the singer's school?
2 Who is in the park?
3 Who is in the USA?
4 Who is in Japan?

**12** Find thirteen names in the song.

Jill, Simon …

# 2 Favourite things

**1** Sam and Kate are in Max's submarine.

Kate  Wow! This is fantastic.
Sam  Look! It's a shark!

**2** They meet Max's friend.

Sam  You've got a lot of computers!
Max  Yes, I have. This is Tess. She's my friend.
Tess  Hello. This is my pet, Tech.
Kate  Hi. I'm Kate. He's Sam.

**3** Sam has got a plan.

Max  Imelda has got my magic crystal. She's in Crystalia.
Kate  Let's go to Crystalia.
Max  I can't go. I haven't got the crystal. It's my power.
Sam  We can go to Crystalia and find the crystal.

**4** Max gives them a magic ring and a key.

Max  Listen! Imelda has got my mobile palace, but I've got a key. And this is a magic ring.
Kate  Fantastic!

**5** Kate and Sam go to Crystalia.

Kate  Magic ring! Take us to Crystalia!

**1** Correct the false sentences. 📼

1 Tess is Max's sister.
2 Tech is Max's pet.
3 Imelda is in Britain.
4 Max gives Sam and Kate a computer.
5 The children go home.

**2** Find words in the story to match the pictures.

①   ②   ③   ④

# Grammar

## have got

| Affirmative | Negative | Interrogative |
|---|---|---|
| I you have/'ve got | I you have not/ haven't got | Have I you got …? |
| he she has/'s got it | he she has not/ hasn't got it | Has he she got …? it |
| we you have/'ve got they | we you have not/ haven't got they | Have we you got …? they |
| **Short answers** | | |
| Yes, I have. | No, he hasn't. | |

**3** Write sentences. Use the correct form of *have got*.

Tom and Daniel/bikes ✓
**Tom and Daniel have got bikes.**

1 Helen/a Walkman ✗
2 They/a PlayStation ✓
3 Anna and Mila/pets ✗
4 I/a PlayStation ✓
5 Alex/a pet ✓
6 Simon and Kathy/computers ✓
7 We/a computer ✗

**4** Complete the dialogue. Use short forms of *have got*.

| | |
|---|---|
| **Tom** | We ¹_____ a new PlayStation at our house. |
| **Harry** | Fantastic! ²_____ you _____ a football game? |
| **Tom** | No, I ³_____ a football game, but my sister ⁴_____ a great James Bond game. |
| **Harry** | What about your brother? ⁵_____ he _____ any games? |
| **Tom** | Yes, he ⁶_____ a fantastic Formula One game. |
| **Harry** | You're lucky! I ⁷_____ a PlayStation. |
| **Tom** | No, but you ⁸_____ a Game Boy. That's really cool. |

# Vocabulary

## Pets

**5** Match the pictures with the words in the box.

tortoise  goldfish  lizard  rabbit  budgie  snake

① ② ③ ④ ⑤ ⑥

# Listening

**6** Sally has got a lot of pets. Listen and choose the correct alternatives. 📼

Jack is from Britain / France.
1 He's *brown / black and white*.
2 Bobby is a *snake / goldfish*.
3 He's *orange / green*.
4 Sally's got *two / three* lizards from Argentina.
5 Sam and Joe are *rabbits / budgies*.
6 Sally's got a *tortoise / snake* from Ecuador.

# Speaking

**7** Tell the class about your pet or your favourite animal.

**I've got a dog. His name's Ben and he's brown.**

## Reading

**1** Look at the pictures. Which countries do you think the children are from?

**2** Read the text and check your answers to exercise 1. 📼

# Favourite things from around the world

**A** My name's Kazu. I'm ten years old and I'm from Tokyo, in Japan. This is my robot dog, Sato. It's just like a real dog! This is my portable DVD player and these are my DVDs. My favourite films are Japanese, but I like American films, too.

**B** My name's Naledi. It means *star* in my language. I'm ten and I'm from Cape Town, in South Africa. This is my bottle cap man. The caps are from cola bottles. My favourite thing is my wooden scooter. It's great! I've also got a pet lizard. It's brown and its name is Oringo.

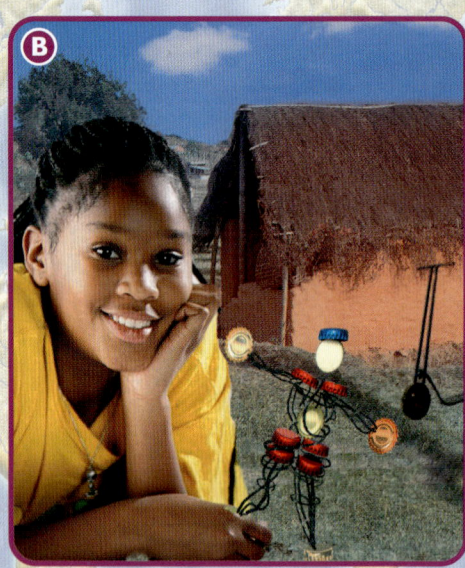

**C** Hi! I'm Harry. I'm eleven and I'm from Nottingham, in Britain. These are my football stickers and my special sticker book. I love football! My favourite team is Liverpool. They're fantastic! I like my Game Boy, too. I've got some great games!

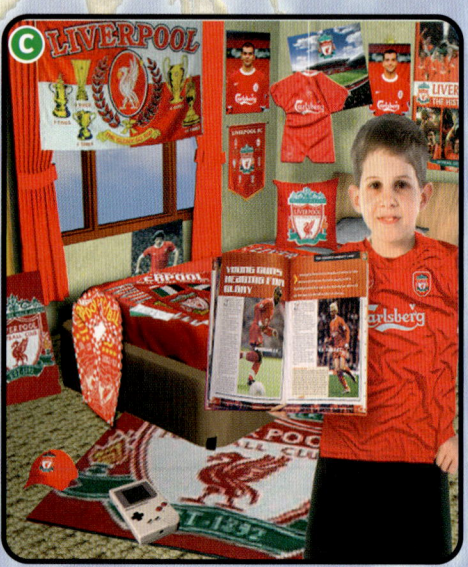

**3** Read the text again and write the correct answers.

| Kazu | Naledi | Harry |
|------|--------|-------|

Who is Japanese? **Kazu**
1 Who is eleven?
2 Who has got a scooter?
3 Who has got a special book?
4 Who is from South Africa?
5 Who is British?
6 Who has got a robot?

**4** Match the pictures with the words from the text.

| scooter | stickers | DVD | cap |
|---------|----------|-----|-----|

**5** Discuss the questions.
1 Who has got the best things?
2 Which things would you like?

# Grammar

### *this*, *that*, *these* and *those*

*this* (singular) + *these* (plural) → near
*that* (singular) + *those* (plural) ⟶ far

This is a DVD.

That's a plane.

These are stickers.

Those are cars.

**6** Complete the dialogues.

**Mel** What are those?
**Tim** They're hats.

**1 Jack** _____?
**Sally** It's a sandwich.

**2 Ann** _____?
**Sue** It's Sarah's pet dog.

**3 Tom** _____?
**Jill** They're shoes.

**4 Nicky** _____?
**Lola** They're houses.

**5 Josh** _____?
**Pete** It's my Game Boy.

# Vocabulary

### Possessions

**7** Match the pictures with the words in the box.

football   skateboard   mobile phone   bike
rollerblades   magazine   watch   Walkman

① ② ③ ④ ⑤ ⑥ ⑦ ⑧

# Speaking

**8** Ask and answer with a partner about things in your classroom.

What's this?

It's a pencil.

What's that?

# Model text

**1** **Read the letter to *Kids' World* magazine and answer the questions.**

1 What's Adam's favourite thing?
2 What's his favourite pet?

Dear Kids' World

My name's Adam. I'm ten years old and I'm from Britain. My favourite thing is my PlayStation. I love it! I've got about ten games. I really like my red skateboard, too. It's fantastic.

I've also got three pets. My dog's name is Coco and my snake is called Cleopatra. They're great. But my favourite pet is Godzilla. She's a lizard!

Adam

**2** **Read the letter again and answer the questions.**

1 How old is Adam?
2 Where's he from?
3 What colour is his skateboard?
4 What pets has he got?
5 What is his snake's name?

# Listening

**3** **Listen to the children's game *Guess the mystery object*. Tick the objects they mention.** 📼

bag ☐
pen ☐
cat ☐
watch ☐
CD ☐
notebook ☐
dog ☐

**4** **Listen again and complete the sentences.** 📼

The mystery object is black and *white*.
1 The mystery object is very _____.
2 Simon hasn't got a _____.
3 His pet is a _____.
4 The mystery object is in the _____.
5 The mystery object is Simon's _____.

# Speaking

**5** **Play *Guess the mystery object* with a partner. Student A thinks of an object in the classroom. Student B tries to guess what it is.**

The mystery object is white.

Is it the board?

No, it isn't. It's small.

Is it your notebook?

Yes, it is.

# Writing

## Punctuation

Always check your punctuation. It can be different in your language.

**6** Match the punctuation marks with their names.

1 My name's Tom**.**          **a** exclamation mark
2 'Are you British**?**'       **b** apostrophe
3 'Yes**,** I am.'             **c** comma
4 It**'**s 5 o'clock.          **d** full stop
5 Hi **!**                     **e** question mark

**7** Rewrite the sentences with the correct punctuation.

1 My names Jenny
2 Ive got a pet cat
3 Its names Joseph
4 Hes fantastic
5 Have you got a pet

**8** Write a letter to *Kids' World* magazine. Tell them about your favourite things. Use the model text and the writing guide to help you.

Dear .....
My name's .....
I'm ..... years old and I'm from .....
I've got .....
My favourite thing is .....
I really like .....

## Song

**9** Listen and complete the song. Use the words in the box.

    fish   hats   pets   boys   girls   pens

# The magic shop

Boys and ¹_____, please come this way
See what's in the shop today
Funny ²_____ and magic rings
And a lot of very special things

They've got ³_____ and purple dogs
They've got snakes and funny frogs
They've got magic ⁴_____ and books
Please come in! Please stop and look!

Magic phones and funny ⁵_____
Robot pets and magic cats
⁶_____ and girls, please come this way
Choose your favourite thing today

open

**10** Complete the puzzle with words from the song. What's the extra word?

1 You can buy things here.
2 Sam and Kate have got a _____ ring.
3 These animals jump and swim.
4 These pets go for walks with you.
5 You wear these on your head.
6 These animals are long and thin.
7 You wear these on your fingers.

# Revision Units 1-2

## Vocabulary

### Countries and nationalities

**1** Complete the sentences.

1 Mary is from the USA. She's _____.
2 Sato is from _____. He's Japanese.
3 Nikos is from Greece. He's _____.
4 Edith is from _____. She's French.
5 Kelly is from Britain. She's _____.
6 Mario is from _____. He's Italian.

### Pets

**2** Write the correct words.

1 _____
2 _____
3 _____
4 _____
5 _____
6 _____

## Possessions

**3** Complete the words with *a*, *e*, *i*, *o* or *u*.

skateb**o**ard

1 b_k_

2 m_g_z_n_

3 W_lkm_n

4 m_b_l_ ph_n_

5 w_tch

6 f_ _tb_ll

7 r_ll_r bl_d_s

## Vocabulary extra

**4** Choose the correct answers.

1 Max is the _____ of Crystalia.
  **a** king   **b** enemy   **c** queen
2 Alina's house is in my street. She's my _____.
  **a** student   **b** favourite   **c** neighbour
3 Oliver is my _____ friend.
  **a** strange   **b** great   **c** best
4 Open the door with your _____.
  **a** key   **b** scooter   **c** ring
5 I've got a great _____ book.
  **a** sticker   **b** bottle   **c** cap

# Grammar

## be: present simple

**5** Complete the dialogues with the correct form of *be*.

**Emily** ¹_____ you American?
**Tom** Yes, I ²_____ . I ³_____ from Los Angeles.

**Josh** ⁴_____ Tim and James in the football team?
**Alex** No, they ⁵_____ . They ⁶_____ in the basketball team.

**Lily** ⁷_____ your scooter red?
**Sarah** No, it ⁸_____ . It ⁹_____ blue.

## Possessive adjectives

**6** Complete the letter with possessive adjectives.

Dear Gina,

Here's a photo of me and ¹_____ classmates.
We really like ²_____ school.
³_____ best friend James is from Scotland.
He's great, Marco is really nice, too. ⁴_____
mum and dad are from Italy. The two girls in the photo
are Nina and Kelly. They live in a very big house
because ⁵_____ mum is a pop star!

Write to me and tell me about ⁶_____ school.

Peter

## Possessive forms

**7** Choose the correct alternatives.

1 My *dad's / dads'* motorbike is very expensive.
2 We've got two cats. Our *cat's / cats'* favourite food is fish!
3 Are those *Susie's / Susies'* stickers?
4 My *friend's / friends'* names are Ben and Matt.
5 My *teacher's / teachers'* hair is brown and her eyes are blue.

## have got

**8** Correct the sentences.

Oliver has got a blue bag.
*Oliver hasn't got a blue bag. He's got a red bag.*

**1** We've got a lot of books.

**2** Amy has got a pet snake.

**3** Helen and her friend have got black hair.

**4** Tekin has got a new computer.

**5** They've got a small dog.

**6** Kelly has got a scooter.

## this, that, these and those

**9** Complete the boy's sentences with *this is*, *that's*, *these are* and *those are*.

*This is* my room.

1 _____ my new computer.
2 _____ my favourite jacket.
3 _____ my football magazines.
4 _____ my rollerblades.
5 _____ my computer games.
6 _____ my David Beckham picture.

# 3 Family

**1** Sam and Kate are in Crystalia.

Sam  Wow! This is amazing!
Kate  Look at the cars!
Sam  Look at the houses!
Kate  Let's talk to those children.

**2** They meet Finn and Star.

Finn  I'm Finn and this is my sister, Star.
Kate  I'm Kate and this is Sam. We're King Max's friends. We want to help him.
Star  He's a good king. Imelda is horrible.
Kate  Where is Imelda?
Finn  Come with us!

**3** They find Imelda.

Finn  Look! There's Imelda.
Star  And that's her mobile palace.
Kate  She's got the crystal!
Sam  Who is he?
Star  His name's Nero. He's Imelda's bodyguard.

**4** Imelda leaves in the mobile palace.

Kate  Wow, Look at those lights!
Sam  The palace can move!
Star  Quick! You can follow Imelda.
Sam  Good idea!
Kate  Come on. Run!

**5** They follow Imelda.

Sam  I'm scared.
Kate  Don't worry, Sam.

**1** Put the events in the story in the correct order.

a  They meet Finn and Star. ☐
b  Imelda leaves. ☐
c  The children arrive in Crystalia. ☐ 1
d  They find Imelda's palace. ☐
e  They follow Imelda. ☐

**2** Match the words from the story with the definitions.

1  amazing (picture 1)       a  Not nice.
2  horrible (picture 2)      b  Go after.
3  follow (picture 4)        c  Frightened.
4  scared (picture 5)        d  Fantastic.

# Grammar

## Present simple (affirmative, spelling)

| Affirmative | 3rd person spelling | | |
|---|---|---|---|
| I you } like | help love | + -s | helps loves |
| he she } likes it | go teach wash guess fix | + -es | goes teaches washes guesses fixes |
| we you } like they | try | + -ies | tries |

**3** Write the third person singular form of the verbs.

1 eat _____
2 finish _____
3 make _____
4 go _____
5 carry _____
6 get up _____
7 tidy _____
8 kiss _____

**4** Complete the sentences. Use the present simple.

**Finn and Star**

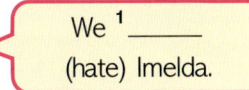
We **1** _____ (hate) Imelda.

**Finn**

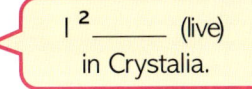
I **2** _____ (live) in Crystalia.

**Sam**

You **3** _____ (play) a lot of sport in Crystalia.

**Star**

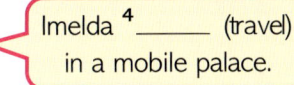
Imelda **4** _____ (travel) in a mobile palace.

**Sam and Kate**

We **5** _____ (want) to help Max.

# Listening

**5** Listen to Lucy and Kate. Choose the correct alternatives.

1 Lucy's dad makes great *pizzas / hamburgers*.
2 Oliver *plays football / watches TV* a lot.
3 Kate hates *football / basketball*.
4 Oliver and his mum like *art / music*.
5 *Lucy / Oliver* goes to the park with Bessie.
6 Bessie is a *lazy / clever* dog.

# Speaking

**6** Guess about your partner's family.

You live in Newton Street.

No, that's wrong. I live in Kennedy Street.

Your brother plays football.

Yes, that's right!

# Writing

**7** Complete the sentences about your family.

1 My mum works …
2 We live …
3 I get up …
4 My mum likes …
5 I play …
6 My dad watches …

# Reading

**1** **Look at the photos of the Flintstones. What do you know about them?**

   **1** Do the Flintstones live in our time?

   **2** Do they have a pet?

   **3** Do they have a baby?

**2** **Read the text and check your answers to exercise 1.**

## Meet the Flintstones!

Do you know the Flintstones? They don't live in our time. They live in the Stone Age! They've got a stone car, a stone TV and even a stone computer!

5  Fred Flintstone loves films and bowling, and he also loves golf. But he doesn't like his job. In fact, he's quite lazy. He's got a lot of crazy plans and he wants to be very rich!

Fred's wife Wilma loves her husband, but she
10 doesn't like his crazy ideas. Wilma doesn't work because she stays at home with their baby daughter Pebbles. She likes music and she plays the piano, too. The Flintstones' pet is a red dinosaur! His name is Dino. When Fred
15 comes home from work, Dino kisses him!

The Flintstones' neighbours are the Rubbles. Barney Rubble works with Fred. His wife Betty is Wilma's best friend. Barney and Betty's son is Bamm-Bamm. He's crazy!

20 The two families are great friends. At the weekends, they go out in their stone car and eat brontosaurus burgers! It's their favourite food!

**3** **Read the text again and choose the correct answers.**

   **1** Fred Flintstone likes …

     **a** his job.  **b** golf.  **c** music.

   **2** Wilma is Fred's …

     **a** daughter.  **b** pet.  **c** wife.

   **3** Dino …

     **a** goes bowling with Fred.

     **b** kisses Fred.

     **c** works with Fred.

   **4** Betty is …

     **a** Wilma's sister.

     **b** Barney's daughter.

     **c** Wilma's friend.

   **5** At weekends, the Rubbles and the Flintstones …

     **a** watch TV.  **b** go out.  **c** play sport.

**4** **Match the words from the text with the definitions.**

   **1** the Stone Age (line 2)    **a** Have a lot of money.

   **2** plans (line 7)    **b** A type of dinosaur.

   **3** rich (line 8)    **c** A time in the past.

   **4** brontosaurus (line 22)    **d** Ideas.

**5** **Discuss the questions.**

   **1** Do you like the Flintstones? Why/Why not?

   **2** Do you know any other TV families?

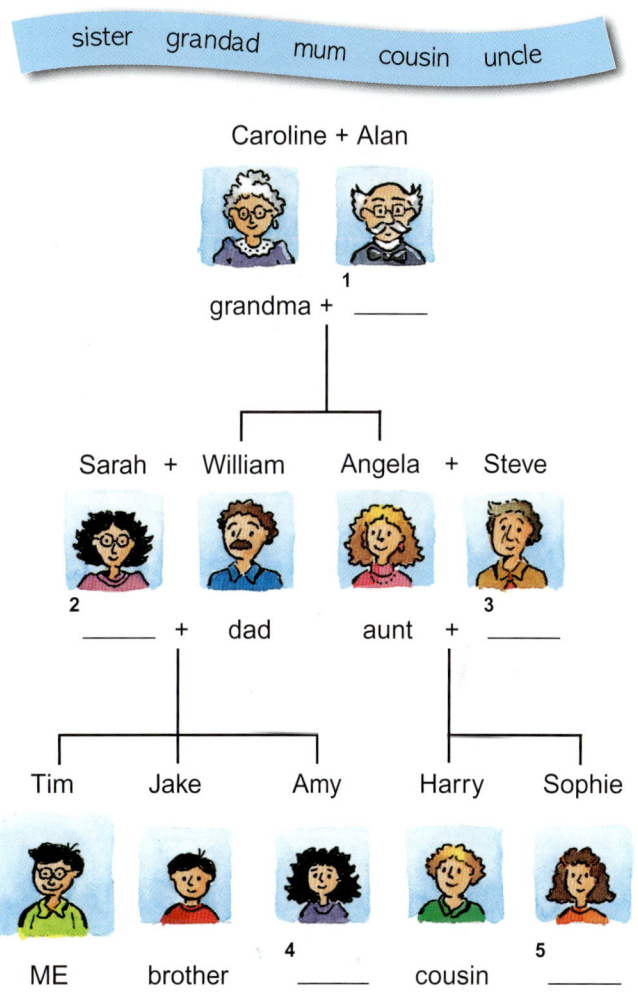 comment: positioned at top-right for lesson marker

# Grammar

## Present simple (negative, interrogative)

| Negative | | Interrogative | | |
|---|---|---|---|---|
| I<br>you | do not like/don't like | Do | I<br>you | like …? |
| he<br>she<br>it | does not like/doesn't like | Does | he<br>she<br>it | like …? |
| we<br>you<br>they | do not like/don't like | Do | we<br>you<br>they | like …? |

**Short answers**

Yes, he does.    No, he doesn't.

**6** **Look at the pictures and correct the sentences.**

Luke reads comics.
**Luke doesn't read comics. He reads books.**

1 Luke and Sarah play football.

2 Sarah supports Manchester United.

3 Luke and Sarah listen to the radio.

4 Luke likes chocolate.

**7** **Write the questions.**

your mum/drive you to school?
**Does your mum drive you to school?**
what sport/you play at school?
**What sport do you play at school?**

1 you/like your teacher?
2 she/give you homework?
3 what time/school/start?
4 you/have lunch at school?
5 where/you go/after school?
6 you/have lessons in the evening?

**8** **Answer the questions in exercise 7.**

# Vocabulary

## Family

**9** **Complete Tim's family tree with the words in the box.**

sister  grandad  mum  cousin  uncle

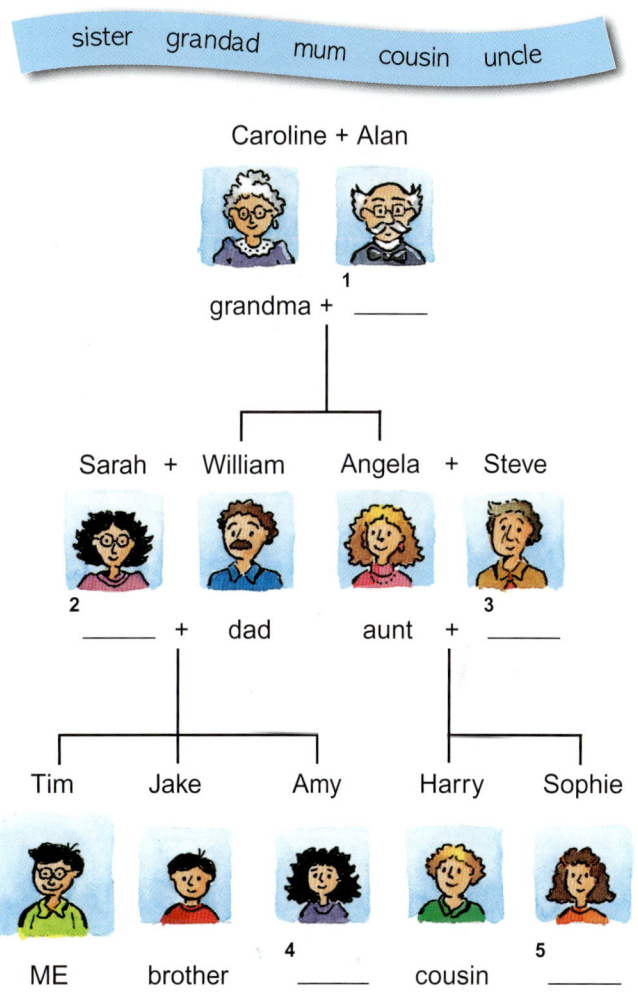

Caroline + Alan

grandma + _____ 1

Sarah + William    Angela + Steve

2            3

_____ + dad    aunt + _____

Tim    Jake    Amy    Harry    Sophie

ME    brother    _____ 4    cousin    _____ 5

Sarah is William's **wife**.
William is Sarah's **husband**.
Amy is William's **daughter**.
Tim is William's **son**.
Amy is Caroline's **granddaughter**.
Harry is Caroline's **grandson**.

# Speaking

**10** **Ask and answer with a partner.**

Who is Tim's grandma?

Caroline.

Tim/grandma
1 Harry/parents
2 Alan/granddaughters
3 Sophie/brother
4 Harry/cousins
5 Angela/husband
6 Amy/grandad

## Model text

**1** **Read the text. Who cooks in Nick's house?**

My family by Nick Winton

I live in a big house with Mum and Dad, my sister and my grandparents.

My sister Julie is a good musician. She plays the guitar and she wants to be a pop star. Julie has got a lot of friends. She goes out a lot, but she doesn't tidy her room.

My mum is a teacher and my dad works in a restaurant. They go to work early. Grandma makes breakfast for us and Grandad takes us to school. In the evening, my dad cooks dinner for us. He's a great cook! After dinner, I watch TV or play cards with Grandad. But he always wins!

**2** **Read the text again. Are the sentences true or false? Correct the false sentences.**

There are five people in Nick's family. **False**
**There are six people in Nick's family.**
1 Nick's house is very small.
2 He lives with his grandparents.
3 His mum doesn't work.
4 Nick's mum cooks dinner.
5 Nick plays cards with his grandma.

## Listening

**3** **Look at the photos of Kelly and Matthew. Do you think they are …**

a friends?
b classmates?
c brother and sister?

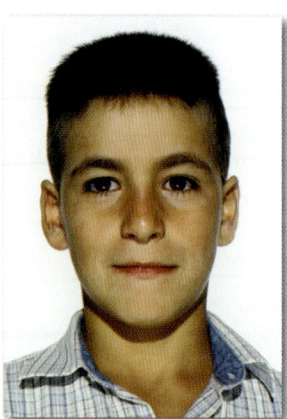

**4** **Listen and check your answer to exercise 3.** 📼

**5** **Listen again and complete the notes.** 📼

Kelly thinks Matthew is a bit **boring**.
1 After school, Matthew does his _____.
2 He loves _____.
3 His room is very _____.
4 Kelly doesn't like _____.
5 She loves her _____.
6 Matthew and Kelly like _____.

## Speaking

**6** **Tell your partner about your family.**

My parents' names are …

I've got two … and one ….

We live in …

My sister likes …

# Writing

## *and*, *but* and *or*

We use *and*, *but* and *or* to join two ideas.

- My sister Jess reads books **and** magazines.
- I watch TV, **but** I don't watch films.
- My brother doesn't like football **or** basketball.
- Do you want to eat pizza **or** pasta tonight?

**7** **Look at the model text on page 26. Underline *and*, *but* and *or*.**

**8** **Complete the sentences with *and*, *but* or *or*.**

1 Is that a dog _____ a cat?
2 I like Jack's brother, _____ I don't like his sister.
3 Do you want burgers _____ pasta?
4 My mum reads newspapers, _____ she doesn't read books.
5 My aunt can play tennis _____ basketball.
6 My cousin likes rap _____ rock music.
7 Do you want to watch the film on Saturday _____ Sunday?

**9** **Write about your family. Use the model text and the writing guide to help you.**

I live in … with my …
I've got … brothers and … sisters
In the morning …
After school / dinner …

# Song

**10** **Listen and choose the correct alternatives.**

## My lazy Saturday

On Saturdays, my mum [1]*gets*/*wakes* up
And washes the kitchen floor
My dad [2]*eats*/*has* breakfast at eight o'clock
And then he cleans the car

My brother [3]*takes*/*has* a long hot shower
And does some work for school
My sister [4]*meets*/*finds* our cousin Ben
Outside the swimming pool

Saturdays are busy days
For them, but not for me
Because I [5]*wake*/*get* up at ten o'clock
And then I watch TV

**11** **Answer the questions.**

Who has breakfast at eight o'clock?
*the singer's dad*
Who likes TV? *the singer*

1 Who cleans the house?
2 Who goes swimming?
3 Who does homework?
4 Who gets up late?

**12** **Find five family words in the song.**

*mum*

# 4 Sport

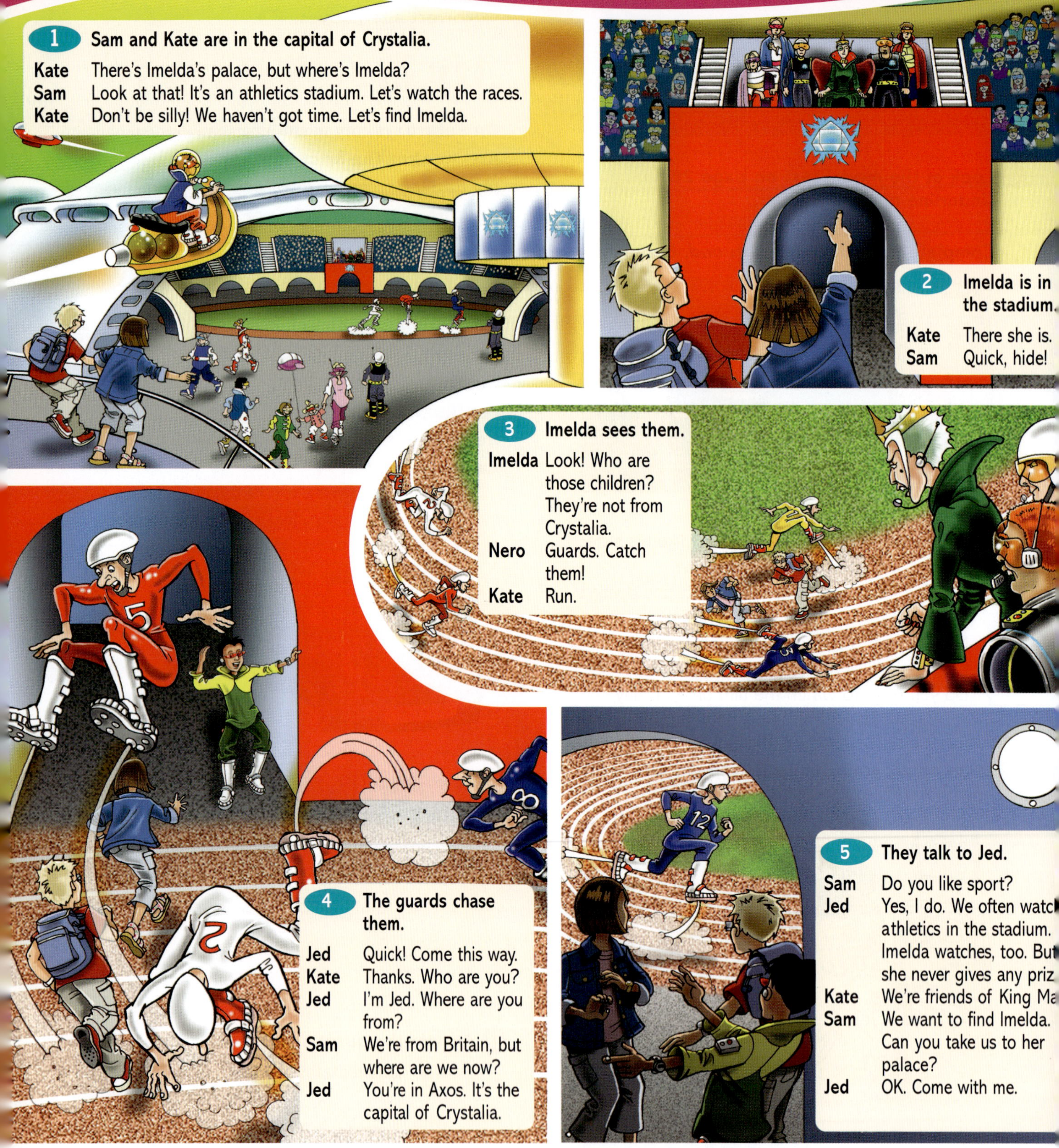

**1** Sam and Kate are in the capital of Crystalia.

Kate There's Imelda's palace, but where's Imelda?
Sam Look at that! It's an athletics stadium. Let's watch the races.
Kate Don't be silly! We haven't got time. Let's find Imelda.

**2** Imelda is in the stadium.

Kate There she is.
Sam Quick, hide!

**3** Imelda sees them.

Imelda Look! Who are those children? They're not from Crystalia.
Nero Guards. Catch them!
Kate Run.

**4** The guards chase them.

Jed Quick! Come this way.
Kate Thanks. Who are you?
Jed I'm Jed. Where are you from?
Sam We're from Britain, but where are we now?
Jed You're in Axos. It's the capital of Crystalia.

**5** They talk to Jed.

Sam Do you like sport?
Jed Yes, I do. We often watch athletics in the stadium. Imelda watches, too. But she never gives any priz
Kate We're friends of King Ma
Sam We want to find Imelda. Can you take us to her palace?
Jed OK. Come with me.

---

**1** Answer the questions.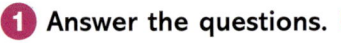

1 What sport do the children see?
2 Where is Imelda?
3 Who chases the children?
4 Who helps them?
5 What's the name of the capital city?

**2** Find words in the story that mean …

1 An important town. [picture 1]
2 A place for sport. [picture 1]
3 Run after. [picture 4]
4 Presents. [picture 5]

# Grammar

## Adverbs of frequency

| always | ▓▓▓▓▓▓▓ |
|---|---|
| usually | ▓▓▓▓▓ |
| often | ▓▓▓ |
| sometimes | ▓▓ |
| never | |

We use adverbs of frequency before the main verb, but after the verb *be*.
I **sometimes** go *swimming at the weekend.*
I'm **never** late for school.

**3** Complete the sentences with adverbs of frequency. Write true information.

1 I _____ play football at the weekend.
2 My dad _____ watches sport on TV.
3 My mum _____ gets up early on Sundays.
4 My best friend _____ plays basketball with me.
5 My teacher _____ drives to school.

## Question words

**What** sports do you like?
**Why** do you like them?
**Where** are you from?
**How** old are you?
**Who** is your favourite football player?
**When** is your birthday?
**Which** school do you go to?
**Whose** book is this?

**4** Put the words in the correct order.

sport what Roberto Carlos play does?
**What sport does Roberto Carlos play?**

1 long how Marathon is a ?
2 next the Olympics are when ?
3 is David Beckham's who wife ?
4 which is country Ronaldo from ?
5 Serena Williams whose sister is ?
6 from Bayern Munich where are?

**5** Ask and answer the questions in exercise 4.

# Listening

**6** Look at the photo of Mary. What sport does she play?

**7** Listen to the interview with Mary and complete the notes. 📼

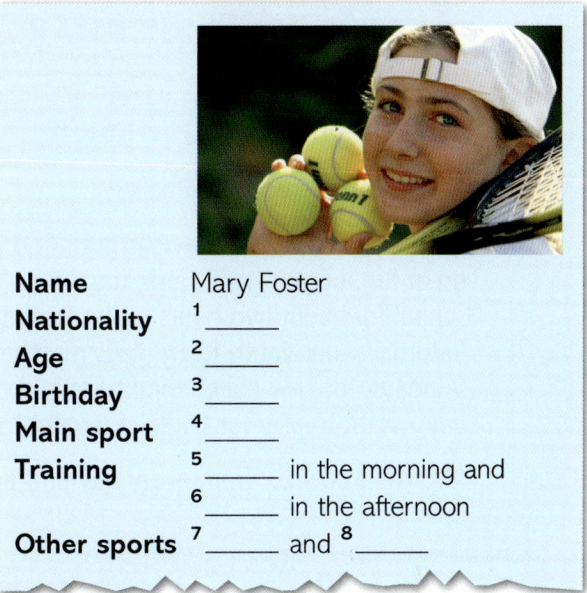

| | |
|---|---|
| **Name** | Mary Foster |
| **Nationality** | [1] _____ |
| **Age** | [2] _____ |
| **Birthday** | [3] _____ |
| **Main sport** | [4] _____ |
| **Training** | [5] _____ in the morning and [6] _____ in the afternoon |
| **Other sports** | [7] _____ and [8] _____ |

# Writing

**8** Write questions to complete the sports survey.

## Sports survey

1 What/your name?
   *What's your name?*

2 When/your birthday?

3 What/your favourite sport?

4 Why/you like it?

5 What sports/you play?

6 What sports/you watch on TV?

7 Who/your favourite sports star?

# Speaking

**9** Ask and answer the questions in exercise 8.

# Reading

**1** Read the text. Whose advice do you agree with? Why? 📼

**Young Sports Stars**

## How can you be successful at sport?
## We ask two young British sports stars for their advice.

**A  Michael Greenwood: footballer.**

I play football for the Newcastle United youth team. It's great fun, but it's hard work, too. I train every day after school for about two hours at the football stadium. On Saturdays, our youth team plays matches. I train on Sundays, too. My coach thinks I'm a good player. One day I want to play for England. I want to be a superstar!

**Michael's advice:** 'Train every day and don't give up!'

**B  Penny Tanner: gymnast**

It isn't easy to be a champion! My dad drives me to the gymnastics club every morning at six a.m. and I train for two hours before school! On Sundays I train all day. My ambition is to go to the Olympics, but I think it's good to have fun, too. On Saturdays I meet my friends, and we often go to the cinema.

**Penny's advice:** 'Don't train all the time. Have some fun!'

**2** Read the text again and answer the questions.

1  Where does Michael train?
2  What does he do on Saturdays?
3  What does he want to do in the future?
4  Where does Penny go before school?
5  How long does she train on Sundays?
6  What does she do with her friends?

**3** Match the words from the text with the definitions.

1  advice [paragraph A]     **a**  A sports teacher.
2  train [paragraph A]     **b**  Good ideas.
3  coach [paragraph A]     **c**  Future plans.
4  champion [paragraph B]     **d**  Practise sport.
5  ambition [paragraph B]     **e**  This person wins prizes.

**4** Would you like to be a famous sports star? Why?/Why not?

# Grammar

## Imperatives and *Let's*

**Imperatives**

We use imperatives to tell someone to do or not do something.
*Train every day!*     *Don't give up!*

**Let's**

We use *Let's* to make a suggestion.
*Let's play football.*

**5** Match the statements with the replies.

| | | | |
|---|---|---|---|
| 1 | It's very expensive. | a | Go to bed! |
| 2 | I'm hungry. | b | Let's watch TV. |
| 3 | It's very hot. | c | Let's have lunch! |
| 4 | I'm tired. | d | Don't buy it! |
| 5 | That's a snake. | e | Open the window! |
| 6 | I'm bored. | f | Don't touch it! |

## Object pronouns

| Subject pronouns | Object pronouns |
|---|---|
| I | me |
| you | you |
| he | him |
| she | her |
| it | it |
| we | us |
| you | you |
| they | them |

**6** Complete the dialogue with the correct subject and object pronouns.

**Sam** What's that?
**Joe** It's a website about the Brazilian football team. Look! There's Ronaldo. Do you like ¹_____?
**Sam** Yeah. ²_____'s fantastic! I like Ronaldinho and Lucio too.
**Joe** ³_____'re on the website, too. And here's an e-mail address for the team.
**Sam** Great! Give ⁴_____ the address. Let's send an e-mail to ⁵_____!

# Vocabulary

## Sports

**7** Match the pictures with the words in the box.

tennis   swimming   basketball   sailing
gymnastics   athletics   ice-skating   karate

We use *play* with ball games.
*I **play** basketball on Fridays.*

We use *go* with sports ending in *–ing*.
*She often **goes** sailing.*

We use *do* with other sports.
*They **do** gymnastics at school.*

# Listening

**8** Listen and write the correct sports.

1 _____   3 _____
2 _____   4 _____

# Speaking

**9** Ask and answer questions about the sports in exercise 7.

What's your favourite sport?

Do you play ...?

# Model text

**1** Read the e-mail. Where are Francisco and Simon from?

Hi, Francisco

I want to tell you about sport in my country. Basketball is very popular here, and it's my favourite sport. My favourite player is Tim Duncan. I like him because he's brilliant! I like American football, too. I often watch games at the Lakers stadium here in Los Angeles.

I don't play basketball or American football because I'm not very tall or strong. But I play ice hockey, and I love skating. Let's go skating when you visit me here in America! It's fun!

Tell me about sport in Argentina!

Simon

**2** Read the e-mail again. Are the sentences true or false? Correct the false sentences.

1 Simon's favourite sport is football.
2 Tim Duncan is a great basketball player.
3 Simon is from Los Angeles.
4 He never plays sport.
5 He wants to go swimming with Francisco.

# Listening

**3** Listen to the *Guess the sports person!* Which sports person does John choose? 📼

**4** Listen again and choose the correct answers. 📼

1 John, Mick and Sarah are …
   **a** sports people.    **b** students.
2 Mick and Sarah can ask John …
   **a** ten questions.    **b** five questions.
3 John's sports person is …
   **a** a man.    **b** a woman.
4 Sarah's favourite sport is …
   **a** basketball.    **b** football.
5 John's sports person lives in …
   **a** Britain.    **b** America.

# Speaking

**5** Play *Guess the sports person!* with a partner. Student A thinks of a sports person. Student B tries to guess who it is.

Is it a woman?

Yes, it is.

Where is she from?

America.

**6** Now change roles and do the activity in exercise 5 again.

# Writing

## because

> We use *because* to give a reason for something.
> *I like him **because** he's brilliant.*
> *Her French is good **because** she lives in Paris.*

**7** Look at the model text on page 32 and underline *because*.

**8** Match the parts of the sentences.

1 I like Formula One racing …
2 Her English is very good …
3 My dad watches the Olympics …
4 I love football …
5 I'm in the school basketball team …
6 John's got two pets …

a because I'm tall.
b because he likes animals.
c because he likes athletics.
d because it's dangerous.
e because her dad is British.
f because the goals are very exciting.

**9** Write true sentences.

1 I often play … because …
2 My favourite sports person is … because …
3 I eat a lot of … because …
4 I like … because …

**10** Write a reply to Simon's e-mail. Write about popular sports in your country. Use the model text and writing guide to help you.

Hi, Simon
… is really popular here.
My favourite player/sports person is
I like him/her because …
I often watch/play …
Let's ….

# Song

**11** Listen and complete the song. Use the words in the box.

sports   time   never   sea   go   always

## Time for me

You ¹_____ train at weekends
On weekdays, you aren't free
You want to be a ²_____ star
You've never got time for me

We never ³_____ to cafés
We never watch TV
We ⁴_____ listen to music
You've never got ⁵_____ for me

You always dream of medals
But I dream of the ⁶_____
Let's go to the beach now
Please give some time to me
Please give some time to me

**12** Answer the questions.
1 What does the singer's friend do on Saturdays and Sundays?
2 What does the singer's friend want to be?
3 Why is the singer sad?
4 What does the singer want to do today?

**13** Look at the song again. Which three words rhyme with *me*?

## Vocabulary

**Family**

**1** Look at the family tree and complete the sentences.

Emma — Mark

Linda — Tim

Lucy — Dan

1 Lucy is Dan's s_____.
2 Linda and Tim are Lucy's p_____.
3 Dan is Linda and Tim's s_____.
4 Linda is Tim's w_____.
5 Lucy is Emma and Mark's g_____.

**2** Find nine more family words in the snake.

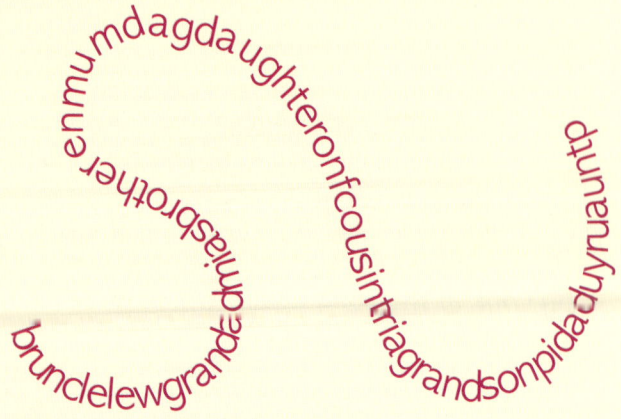

## Sports

**3** Complete the words with *a, e, i, o* or *u*.

1 _c_ sk_t_ng

2 t_nn_s

3 _thl_t_cs

4 gymn_st_cs

5 sw_mm_ng

6 k_r_t_

7 b_sk_tb_ll

8 s_ _ l_ng

## Vocabulary extra

**4** Complete the sentences with the words in the box.

| ambition | capital | prize | rich | scared |

1 I'm _____ of sharks! I don't like them.
2 _____ people have got a lot of money.
3 The _____ of Turkey is Ankara.
4 She's got a _____ because she's the winner of the race.
5 My _____ is to be a sports star.

# Grammar

## Present simple (affirmative and negative)

**5** Complete the sentences. Use the correct form of the present simple.

1 I _____ (play) football in the school team.
2 We _____ (love) football, but our team isn't very good.
3 The coach _____ (shout) at us.
4 The players _____ (not listen) to the coach.
5 Our team _____ (not win) many matches!

## Present simple (interrogative)

**6** Write questions and short answers.

Alice/get up/early? ✔

*Does Alice get up early?*
*Yes, she does.*

1 Lisa's brother/eat/pasta? ✘
2 Tim/like/sport? ✔
3 your grandma/live/near here? ✘
4 you/tidy/your bedroom? ✔
5 Billy and Mark/support/Manchester United? ✘

## Adverbs of frequency

**7** Choose the correct alternatives.

Rosie and Vicky are good friends. They love music so they <sup>1</sup>*usually / never* listen to CDs after school. They're good students and they <sup>2</sup> *always / sometimes* work hard. They <sup>3</sup> *never / often* do their homework together, but not every day. They <sup>4</sup> *often / never* meet at the weekend because Vicky visits her grandparents. But on Sunday evenings, they <sup>5</sup> *always / never* talk on their mobile phones!

## Imperatives and *Let's*

**8** Match the pictures with the sentences in the box.

Let's watch football.     Take off your shoes!
Tidy your bedroom!     Don't play that music!
Let's swim to the island.     Get up!

## Object pronouns

**9** Complete the sentences with the correct subject and object pronouns.

1 I don't like cats. Do you like _____?
2 There's Mark. Let's ask _____.
3 This is my sister. _____ 's six.
4 Can you help _____ with my homework, please?
5 That's a great CD. Let's buy _____.
6 Our parents always take _____ to school.
7 Ellie and Laura are my cousins. _____ live in Scotland.
8 She's from London. We really like _____.

# 5 Home

**1** Jed helps Sam and Kate.

**Kate** Look at Jed!
**Sam** He can run like an athlete.
**Kate** Come on! Let's go into the palace.

**2** They enter the mobile palace.

**3** They're in the living room.

**Imelda** Who are you? Why are you here?
**Kate** Er ... we want to see your beautiful palace.
**Imelda** I don't believe you. I think you're Max's friends.
**Sam** Er ... no. What's that on the table?
**Imelda** It's my magic crystal. You mustn't touch it!

**4** Nero can fly!

**Kate** What can the crystal do?
**Imelda** Watch. Crystal! Show me your power. Fly, Nero!
**Nero** Help!

**5** Kate can't use the crystal.

**Sam** Quick, Kate. Take the crystal!
**Kate** Crystal! You must show me your power. Fly, Imelda!
**Imelda** Ha! Ha! Ha! That's the wrong spell. Catch them, Nero!
**Nero** I can't come down!

**6** They escape.

**Nero** Ouch!
**Imelda** Get up, Nero. Catch the children!
**Sam** Quick! We must escape!
**Kate** Ring, take us to Max!

**1** Correct the false sentences.

1 Jed goes into the palace.
2 Imelda and Nero are in the stadium.
3 Imelda believes the children.
4 Kate can fly.
5 Imelda and Nero catch the children.

**2** Match the words from the story with the definitions.

1 enter (picture 2)
2 beautiful (picture 3)
3 fly (picture 4)
4 spell (picture 5)
5 escape (picture 2)

a Run away.
b Magic words.
c Very nice.
d Birds can do this.
e Go into.

# Grammar

## Modal verbs: *can* and *must*

**can**

We use *can* to talk about ability.

He **can** run.          Kate **can't** use the crystal.

**Can** you swim?          Yes, I **can**./No, I **can't**.

We use *can* to ask for and give permission.

**Can I** have some chocolate?

**must and mustn't**

We use *must* when we talk about obligation.

We use *mustn't* when we aren't allowed to do something.

We **must** escape.     You **mustn't** touch it!

**3** Complete the sentences. Use *can* and *can't*.

1  The guards _____ catch Jed.
2  Max's key _____ open the palace door.
3  Imelda _____ use the magic crystal.
4  Nero _____ fly.
5  Kate _____ say the magic spell.
6  Sam and Kate _____ take the crystal to Max.

**4** Complete the dialogue with *must* or *mustn't*.

**Mum** Lucy! You ¹_____ finish your homework!

**Lucy** Oh, Mum! Can I go to Ricky's house?

**Mum** Yes, you can. But you ²_____ finish your homework before you go. And you ³_____ telephone me when you arrive at his house.

**Lucy** OK, Mum.

**Mum** And you ⁴_____ come home at eight o'clock. You ⁵_____ go to bed early.

**Lucy** OK Mum. Can I go now?

**Mum** Wait! It's cold. You ⁶_____ forget your jacket!

# Vocabulary

## Bedroom objects

**5** Match the pictures with the words in the box.

curtains  carpet  shelf  desk  wardrobe  bed

# Listening

**6** Listen to the conversation between Nick and his mum. Are the sentences true or false? 📼

1  Nick must leave his football boots on the carpet.
2  He must clean them.
3  He can tidy his room later.
4  He must put his clothes in the wardrobe.
5  He can watch TV now.
6  He mustn't go to Kelly's house.

# Speaking

**7** What rules have you got in your house? Tell the class.

> I can't watch TV before I do my homework.

## Reading

**1** Look at the photos. Which house would you like to visit?

**2** Read the article and match the photos with the paragraphs. 📼

# Crazy houses!

**There are a lot of different types of houses in the world. But these three houses are very unusual ...**

**A** The *Shoe House* is like a shoe. There are pictures of shoes on the windows and doors, and the letter box is a shoe, too. The house isn't very big, but there are three bedrooms and two bathrooms. The address? Shoe House Road!

**B** This isn't a spaceship – it's a *Futuro House*! These amazing houses have got a lot of windows, and four legs! The house has got plastic walls, and all the furniture is plastic, too. There aren't any bedrooms, but eight people can sleep in the house. Special chairs in the living room become beds at night. They're very comfortable!

**C** This strange house is 125 years old, and it's called *Lucy the Elephant*. People don't live in it now because it's a museum. The doors of the house are in the elephant's feet, and the stairs are in the elephant's legs. Its eyes are two round windows!

**3** Read the text again and write the name of the houses.

> Lucy the Elephant    A Futuro House
> The Shoe House

This house is 125 years old. **Lucy the Elephant**
1 There are two bathrooms in this house.
2 This house is a museum.
3 This house has got plastic walls.
4 The windows of this house are like eyes.
5 There are three bedrooms in this house.
6 There are special chairs in this house.

**4** Find words in the text to match the definitions.

1 Your house number, street, and town. [paragraph A]
2 A type of material. [paragraph B]
3 You stand on these. [paragraph B]
4 You climb up these. [paragraph C]
5 Like a circle. [paragraph C]

**5** Would you like to live in one of these houses? Why?/Why not?

# Grammar

## there is / there are

| Singular | Plural |
| --- | --- |
| *There is*/*There's* a letter box. | *There are* three bedrooms. |
| *There isn't* a garage. | *There aren't* any windows. |
| *Is there* a bathroom? | *Are there* any shelves? |
| Yes, *there is.* | Yes, *there are.* |
| No, *there isn't.* | No, *there aren't.* |

**6** Complete the dialogue with the correct form of *there is/there are*.

**Sally** What's your new house like?

**Tom** It's great! ¹_____ three bedrooms. I like my room a lot. ²_____ a computer and ³_____ a lot of shelves for all of my CDs.

**Sally** ⁴_____ a garden?

**Tom** Yes, ⁵_____. It's very big. And ⁶_____ a swimming pool. You can come to my house and swim!

**Sally** Great! Thanks, Tom.

## Prepositions of place

**7** Match the pictures with the words in the box.

in   on   in front of   behind
between   opposite   under   next to

# Vocabulary

## Places in a house

**8** Match the words in the box with the places.

balcony   bathroom   bedroom   dining room
garden   hall   kitchen   living room

# Speaking

**9** Look at the picture in exercise 8 for one minute. Then ask and answer questions.

Where's the robot?

It's in the hall.

Where's the black cat?

# Writing

**10** Write about your house or flat.

I live in a flat. It's got four rooms. There's a ...

# Model text

**1** Read the text. Does Beth like her bedroom?

## My bedroom

My bedroom is opposite my sister's room, and it's really big!

I've got a comfortable bed and I've also got a nice desk. The desk is in front of the window so I do my homework there. There are three long shelves next to my desk. I put my books and CDs on them. There are some great posters of my favourite pop singers and film stars on the walls.

It's a really nice bedroom, but I don't like the horrible pink carpet. I hate pink!

**2** Read the text again and answer the questions.

1 Where is Beth's bedroom?
2 Where does she do her homework?
3 What does she put on her shelves?
4 What posters are there on her walls?
5 Why doesn't she like the carpet?

# Listening

**3** Listen to Teri and Khayam. Who shares a bedroom? 📼

**4** Listen again and complete the sentences. 📼

Teri's family live **underground**.
1 There are four _____ in Teri's house.
2 Her bedroom has got a bed, a wardrobe and two _____.
3 There aren't any _____ in her bedroom.
4 There are two bedrooms in Khayam's _____.
5 Khayam's family must _____ the tent every day.
6 He sleeps on a _____.

# Speaking

**5** Ask and answer with a partner.

How big is your bedroom?

What furniture have you got?

Is there a ... in your bedroom?

Have you got a ...?

# Writing

## Using adjectives

We use adjectives to make writing more interesting.

I've got a computer game. ➡ I've got an **exciting** computer game.

There's a park near our house. ➡ There's a **nice** park near our house.

**6** Look at the model text on page 40 and underline the adjectives.

**7** Rewrite the paragraph to make it more interesting. Choose some of the adjectives from the box.

~~new~~ boring comfortable fantastic horrible old nice big noisy small amazing

There's a new Internet café in our street.

There's an Internet café in our street. It's got two rooms. You can play computer games and there are posters on the walls. The café sells sandwiches and pizzas. There are a lot of kids there, too!

**8** Write about your bedroom. Use the model text and the writing guide to help you.

My bedroom is ...
There's / There are ...
I've got a ...
There are a lot of ...
There are/is... on the walls/floor

# Song

**9** Listen and complete the song. Use the words in the box. 📼

pink    house    big    good    windows    ears

## *The crazy house*

There's a crazy <sup>1</sup>_____ in the middle of the wood
It's really strange, but it's really <sup>2</sup>_____
It's like a spaceship
Its <sup>3</sup>_____ are round
And sometimes you can hear a humming sound

Crazy house, crazy house
Crazy house in the middle of the wood

There's a crazy creature in this crazy place
It's got a <sup>4</sup>_____ body and a purple face
It's got four huge <sup>5</sup>_____
And one <sup>6</sup>_____ eye
It hasn't got wings, but I think it can fly

Crazy house, crazy house
Crazy house in the middle of the wood (x 2)

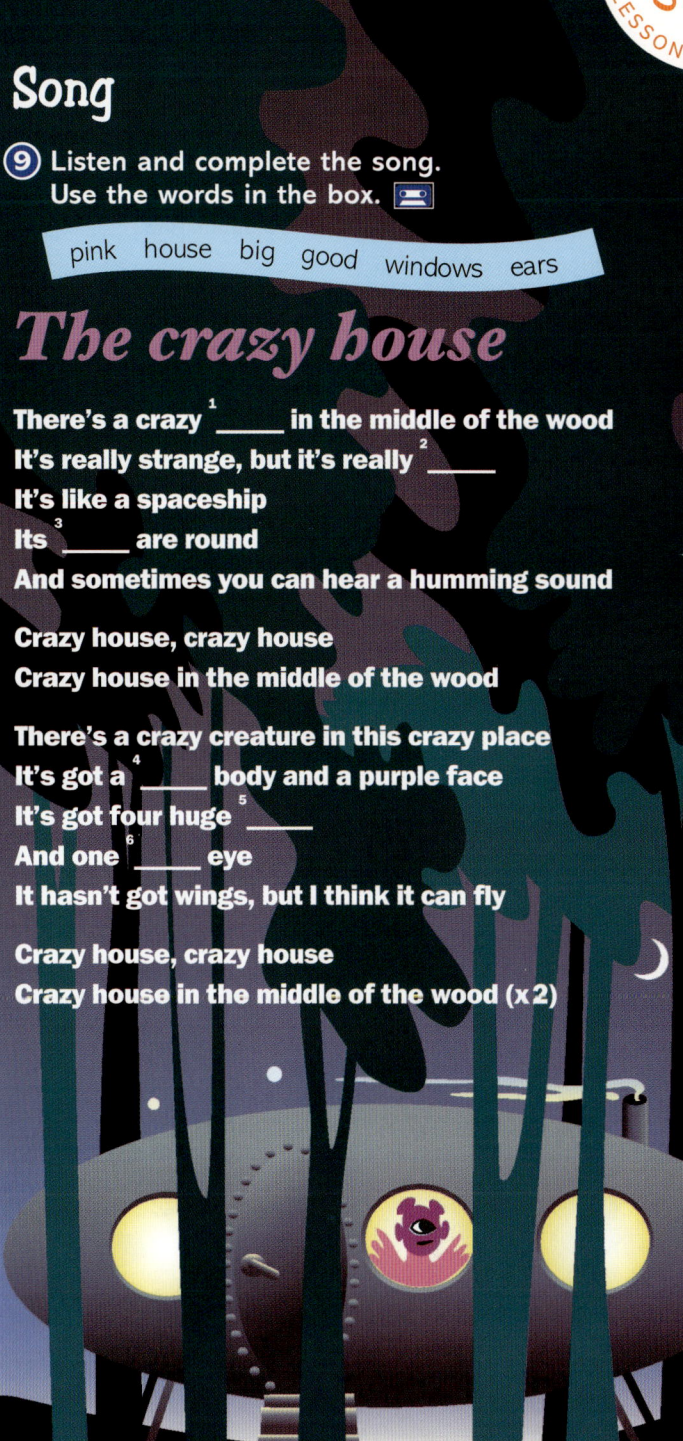

**10** Answer the questions.

1 Where is the house?
2 Who lives in it?
3 Would you like to go there?

**11** Match the words from the song with the definitions.

1 wood (verse 1)      a An animal.
2 spaceship (verse 1)  b There are a lot of trees here.
3 creature (verse 2)   c Birds have these.
4 wings (verse 2)      d Aliens travel in this.

# 6 Parties

**1** **Sam and Kate return to Max's submarine.**

Tess    Sam! Kate! You're back!
Max    Have you got the crystal?
Sam    Er ... no, we haven't.
Kate    Sorry, Max. Don't worry. We can try again.
Max    OK, but first you must rest.

**2** **They don't like Max's food.**

Max    Do you want some lemonade?
Kate    Yes, please.
Max    How about a seaweed biscuit?
Sam    Er .. no thanks. Have you got any crisps?
Max    No, but I've got some really nice octopus sandwiches.
Sam    Oh ... er ... no, thanks.

**3** **Tess gives them some magic presents.**

Tess    Here are some special presents for you.
Kate    Thank you.
Sam    I've got some magic seeds. What have you got, Kate?
Kate    Well .... I've got a hat.
Tess    It's a very special magic hat. Watch!

**4** **Tess is invisible.**

Sam    Wow! I can't see Tess.
Kate    That's amazing!

**5** **They go back to Crystalia.**

Kate    What shall we do now?
Sam    Let's go back to Crystalia and find Imelda.
Kate    All right. Ring! Take us to Crystalia.
Tess    Be careful!

**1** **Correct the false sentences.** 📼

1 Sam and Kate have got the crystal.
2 Sam likes octopus sandwiches.
3 Sam and Kate give Tess a present.
4 Max becomes invisible.
5 Sam and Kate go home.

**2** **Find words in the story to match the pictures.**

①  ②  ③  ④

# Grammar

## Countable and uncountable nouns

We use countable nouns in singular and plural forms.
*She's got an **apple** and two **oranges**.*

We use uncountable nouns in the singular form only.
*Can I have some **water**?*

We use *there is* and *there are* with countable nouns and *there is* with uncountable nouns.

*There's some milk in the fridge.*
*There's a pen in my bag and **there are** two pens in the desk.*

**3** Complete the table with the words in the box.

> apple   milk   sugar   butter   orange   egg

| Countable nouns | | Uncountable nouns |
|---|---|---|
| singular | plural | singular only |
| *apple* | *apples* | *milk* |

## some and any

**some**

We use *some* in affirmative sentences.
*I've got **some** magic seeds.*

**any**

We use *any* in negative sentences and questions.
*We haven't got **any** coffee.    Have you got **any** crisps?*

**4** Complete the dialogue. Use *some* and *any*.

**Kim**  I'm hungry. Is there ¹_____ bread?
**Joe**  Yes, there is. But there isn't ²_____ butter.
**Kim**  OK. Have you got ³_____ eggs?
**Joe**  Yes. There are ⁴_____ eggs in the fridge. Let's make a cheese omelette.
**Kim**  Well ... We've got ⁵_____ milk, but we haven't got ⁶_____ cheese.
**Joe**  Oh! Well, let's go to the café and have a hamburger.

# Vocabulary

## Things for a party

**5** Match the pictures with the words in the box.

> crisps   cake   candles   decorations   present   card

# Speaking

**6** Look at the picture for one minute. Then close your book and ask and answer questions.

> Are there any crisps on the table?

> Yes, there are.

> Are there any cards on the shelf?

> No, there aren't.

# Writing

**7** Write sentences about the picture.

*There's some sugar.*

# Reading

**1** Look at the photos. Which countries do you think they are from?

**2** Read the text and check your answers to exercise 1. 📼

## Festivals from around the world

**How much do you know about festivals in different countries? There are hundreds of amazing celebrations around the world. Here are three of our favourites.**

**A** In August, thousands of people in Buñol, Spain celebrate the festival of *La Tomatina*. The festival begins with fireworks and a parade. Later, people stand in the streets and throw tomatoes at their friends and neighbours. How many tomatoes do they throw? About 125,000 kilos! That's a lot of tomatoes. It's great fun!

**B** Every year in February or March, people in Venice, Italy celebrate the *Carnival*. They wear fantastic costumes and masks and have colourful parades in the narrow streets of the city. There are parties all round the city, and people sing and dance in the streets. One of the biggest parties is in St. Mark's Square. You can go to the square and celebrate with thousands of people. But don't forget your costume and your mask!

**C** In Vietnam in September or October, people celebrate *Trung Thu*, the festival of the moon. On this day, children carry beautiful lanterns through the streets. They also wear colourful masks and eat traditional *moon cakes*. Moon cakes are special rice cakes, and they're delicious!

**3** Read the text again and complete the notes.

### World Festivals

| Name | La Tomatina, Spain | Venice Carnival, Italy | 5 _____, Vietnam |
|---|---|---|---|
| When | August | 2 _____ or 3 _____ | 6 _____ or October |
| What do people do? | They throw 1 _____. | People wear 4 _____. | They wear masks and eat 7 _____. |

**4** Match the pictures with the words in the box.

> fireworks   masks   lantern   costume

**5** What's your favourite festival? Why?

# Grammar

## *How much ... ?* and *How many ... ?*

> We use *How many ...?* with countable nouns.
> *How many* tomatoes do they throw?
>
> We use *How much...?* with uncountable nouns.
> *How much* rice do they eat?

**6** Complete the questions. Use *How much ...?* or *How many ...?* Then answer them.

1 _____ fruit do you eat every day?
2 _____ hamburgers do you eat every month?
3 _____ water do you drink every day?
4 _____ chocolates do you eat at the weekend?
5 _____ cans of cola do you have every week?
6 _____ milk do you drink every day?

## *a lot of*, *a little* and *a few*

> We use *a lot of* with countable and uncountable nouns.
> That's *a lot of* tomatoes!    He's got *a lot of* money.
>
> We use *a little* with uncountable nouns.
> There's *a little* milk in the fridge.
>
> We use *a few* with countable nouns.
> I've got *a few* decorations for the party.

**7** Look at the shopping trolley and write sentences. Use *a lot of*, *a little* and *a few*.

sweets
*There are a lot of sweets in the trolley.*

1 water          4 apples
2 bananas        5 oranges
3 milk

# Vocabulary

## Food

**8** Match the pictures with the words in the box.

> beef    chicken    bananas    lemons
> fruit juice    carrots    potatoes    pasta    coffee

① ② ③
④ ⑤ ⑥
⑦ ⑧ ⑨

# Listening

**9** Listen to Lisa and Mark. What is Lisa's recipe for? 📼

**10** Listen again. Are the sentences true or false? 📼

1 It's Lisa's birthday.
2 There isn't any sugar.
3 There's a little butter.
4 There are six eggs in the fridge.
5 The children decide to buy a cake.

# Speaking

**11** Ask and answer questions about food.

> Do you like bananas?

> How much fruit do you eat?

## Model text

**1** Look at the text and the photo. Is it …

a a letter    b an advert    c an e-mail

# Carnival Time

Come to the Rio Carnival, in Brazil. It's fantastic!

1 Thousands of people watch the carnival every year. Performers wear colourful costumes and dance to samba music. Other people ride on spectacular floats. It lasts for three days!

2 Don't miss the samba schools' parade! The people in the parade make special costumes and floats for the event. After the parade, the schools win prizes for the best floats, songs and dances.

3 There are big parties too. The Copacabana Palace has a very special party and lots of film stars and pop singers go.

**For more information, visit the Rio carnival website.**

**2** Read the text again and answer the questions.

1 How often is the carnival in Rio?
2 What kind of music is popular there?
3 What do people make for the samba schools' parade?
4 What happens after the parade?
5 What happens at the Copacabana Palace?

## Listening

**3** Listen to the interview. What do Karina and Paulo do at the carnival?

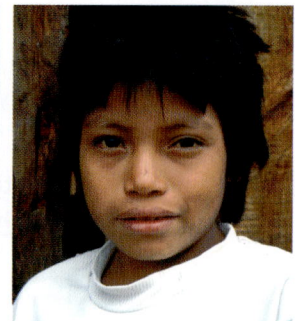

**4** Listen again and choose the correct answers.

1 Karina dances …
   a on a float.
   b in the street.
2 Every samba school has got special …
   a dances.
   b colours.
3 Karina's costume is …
   a orange and green.
   b green and pink.
4 Every samba school has got about eighty
   a drummers.
   b students.
5 At the carnival, Paulo usually…
   a walks with the dancers.
   b watches the parade.

## Speaking

**5** Think about a festival in your country. Ask and answer with a partner.

What's your favourite festival?

How do you celebrate it?

Who do you celebrate with?

What do you wear?

What do you eat?

# Writing

## Writing in paragraphs

Divide your writing into paragraphs. Each paragraph must have a different topic.

**6** Look at the model text on page 46. Which paragraph ...
- **a** describes what people eat?
- **b** introduces the carnival?
- **c** describes one event at the carnival?

**7** Read the advert and divide it into three paragraphs. What's the topic of each paragraph?

### Party in London!

Come to the Notting Hill Carnival, in London. The carnival is in August, and more than a million people enjoy two days of great fun! Don't miss the carnival parade on Sunday. Thousands of children wear colourful costumes and ride on fantastic floats. They make the costumes at school. You can listen to all kinds of music at the festival. Calypso is a very popular traditional music from the Caribbean, but there are also a lot of great pop bands.

**8** Write an advert for a festival in your country. Use the model text and the writing guide to help you. Divide your advert into 3 paragraphs.

Come to ...
Every year ...
It lasts for...
Don't miss ...
... is very popular
You can also ...

# Song

**9** Listen and choose the correct alternatives. 📼

## The party

There are sandwiches and [1] *crisps/cakes*,
  chocolates and sweets
There's a [2] *lovely/birthday* cake
  and a lot of other treats

Come on now! Let's celebrate!
Come on now! Please don't be late!

There are [3] *people/presents*, cards
  and a lot of red balloons
There are decorations
  all around the [4] *room/place*

Come on now! Let's celebrate!
Come on now! Please don't be late!

There's a [5] *drummer/singer*
  and a band and flashing lights
You can listen to great [6] *music/CDs*
  here tonight

Come on now! Let's celebrate!
Come on now! Please don't be late! (x3)

**10** Complete the puzzle with words from the song. What's the extra word?

1. You make these from potatoes.
2. You eat this on your birthday.
3. You give these things to people.
4. A pop group.
5. These things are round and colourful.
6. These things have got a lot of sugar.
7. You can listen to this.

## Vocabulary
### Bedroom objects

**1** Write the correct words.

1
2
3
4
5
6

### Places in a house

**2** Complete the crossword.

**Down**

1 Dad is making pizza in the k_____ .
2 Rosie is cleaning her teeth in the b_____ .
3 We've got two sofas and a big TV in our
  l_____ .
4 There are some beautiful flowers in our
  g_____ .

**Across**

2 Tidy your b_____, Matt!
5 We take off our shoes and jackets in the
  h_____ .
6 We've got a really big dinner table in our
  d_____ .
7 I often sit on the b_____ and watch
  people in the street.

## Things for a party

**3** Complete the words with *a, e, i, o* and *u*.

1 pr_s_nt
2 d_c_r_t_ _ns
3 c_k_
4 cr_sps
5 c_ndl_s
6 c_rd.

## Food

**4** Write the correct words.

1 _____
2 _____
3 _____
4 _____
5 _____
6 _____
7 _____
8 _____
9 _____

## Vocabulary extra

**5** Choose the odd word out.

  fly  escape  seeds  run

1 spell  living room  magic  crystal
2 windows  doors  world  stairs
3 legs  eyes  round  feet
4 octopus  fish  present  seaweed
5 moon  fireworks  costumes  masks

# Grammar

## can and must

**6** Complete the text with the correct form of *can*, *can't*, *must* and *mustn't*.

> **Grafton Museum – Information for visitors**
>
> Welcome to the Museum! You ¹_____ visit us from Monday to Friday. Unfortunately you ²_____ visit at the weekends because the museum is closed.
>
> Visitors ³_____ be quiet in the Museum. They ⁴_____ have picnic lunches in the Museum gardens. But they ⁵_____ leave any rubbish there.
>
> **Enjoy your visit to the Grafton Museum!**

## Prepositions of place

**7** Complete the sentences with the words from the box.

> behind   between   *in*   in front of
> next to   on   opposite   under

**1** There's a goldfish _____ the aquarium.

**2** Our cat always sits _____ an old carpet.

**3** There's a tree _____ our house.

**4** The bank is _____ the CD shop.

**5** Lisa sits _____ me in class.

**6** Our school is _____ the park and the café.

**7** The dog is _____ the table.

**8** Tim's pet snake is _____ the chair.

## Countable and uncountable nouns

**8** Complete the table with the words in the box.

> banana  beef  biscuit  cola  egg  salt
> hamburger  milk  pasta  potato  tomato  water

| Countable noun | | Uncountable noun |
| singular | plural | singular only |
| --- | --- | --- |
| banana | bananas | beef |

## there is/there are, some and any

**9** Look at the picture and write sentences.

rice    *There's some rice.*
chips   *There aren't any chips.*

**1** pizzas          **4** sandwiches
**2** apples          **5** coffee
**3** orange juice    **6** pasta

## How much …?/How many …?

**10** Choose the correct alternative.

**1** Sam's rich! *How much / How many* money has he got?

**2** *How much / How many* homework do you do at the weekend?

**3** Your house is really nice. *How much / How many* bedrooms has it got?

**4** This class is very noisy. *How much / How many* students are there?

**5** *How much / How many* brothers and sisters have you got?

# 7 School

**1** Sam and Kate return to Crystalia.

**Kate** Where are we? Are we in Crystalia?
**Sam** Yes, we're in Axos.
**Kate** Look! Imelda's palace is leaving. What can we do now?
**Sam** Let's find Jed. He can help us.

**2** They find Jed.

**Kate** Look! There's Jed. He's sitting on that bench.
**Sam** Can he see you?
**Kate** No. He isn't looking at us. Come on!
**Sam** Be careful. Look at the guards!

**3** Jed tells them about Megan.

**Jed** Hello! The guards are looking for you.
**Kate** Well ... We're looking for Imelda.
**Sam** Is that a story book?
**Jed** No. It's my maths homework.
**Sam** Yuck! I hate maths, but I like art and music.
**Kate** Where's Imelda, Jed?
**Jed** I don't know, but you can ask Megan. I can take you to her.

**4** Jed takes them to Megan's cave.

**Kate** Who's Megan?
**Jed** She's a wise old woman. She knows everything. She live in this cave.
**Sam** Look! The guards!
**Jed** You must go in.

**5** They go into the cave.

**Jed** Goodbye. I must go now.
**Kate** Bye, Jed. Come on, Sam.
**Sam** It's very scary!

**1** Answer the questions. 📼

1 Who do Sam and Kate look for?
2 Where do they find him?
3 What are Sam's favourite subjects?
4 Who is Megan?
5 Where do Sam and Kate go?

**2** Match the words from the story with the definitions.

1 bench (picture 2)
2 subject (picture 3)
3 wise (picture 4)
4 cave (picture 4)

a Maths or English.
b A dark place.
c You sit on this.
d Very clever.

# Grammar

## Present continuous (affirmative, negative)

|  | Affirmative | Negative |  |
|---|---|---|---|
| I | am/'m | am not/'m not | sleeping |
| you | are/'re are | not/aren't | sitting |
| he she it | is/'s | is not/isn't | learning |
| we you they | are/'re | are not/aren't | eating |

**Spelling**

| look | looking |
|---|---|
| make | making |
| lie + -ing | lying |
| run | running |

**3** Write the correct *-ing* forms.

| smile | **smiling** | tie | 4 _____ |
|---|---|---|---|
| go | 1 _____ | begin | 5 _____ |
| swim | 2 _____ | throw | 6 _____ |
| play | 3 _____ | dance | 7 _____ |

**4** Look at the picture and complete the sentences. Use the present continuous affirmative.

1 Sam and Kate _____ (talk) to Jed.
2 They _____ (ask) him questions.
3 Jed _____ (sit) on a bench.
4 Sam _____ (wear) a red T-shirt.
5 Two children _____ (play) basketball.
6 The guards _____ (look for) Sam and Kate.

**5** Look at the pictures and correct the sentences. Use the words in the box.

> eat chocolate    listen to music    read
> walk    play a game    play basketball

She's cycling
**She isn't cycling.**
**She's walking.**

1 He's listening to the teacher.

2 They're reading.

3 They're doing an exam.

4 He's sleeping.

5 He's drinking cola.

# Speaking

**6** Look at the picture. What are the students doing?

# Writing

**7** Write sentences about the students in exercise 6.

# Reading

**1** Read the text. What is special about Becky's school?

# The School of the Air

Are you sitting in a classroom with your classmates? Is a teacher helping you? Well, some Australian children can't go to a normal school. They study at home!

Australia is a huge country and some children live on very big farms. They can't go to a normal school because the local town is very far away! They study at home with the *School of the Air*.

*School of the Air* students have lessons with a teacher by radio. Some students also use the Internet and video cameras to talk to their teacher and classmates. About three times a year, the students meet their teachers and classmates at a school camp. They have lessons at the camp, but they also play sport.

Becky is eleven years old, and she's a *School of the Air* student. 'It's cool!' she says. 'I don't sit in a classroom all day. At the moment I'm studying for exams with my radio teacher. I'm also doing a lot of work on the Internet. But I miss my classmates. And some lessons are very difficult by radio: especially art lessons and science experiments!'

**2** Answer the questions.

1 Where do *School of the Air* students study?
2 How do the students have lessons?
3 How often do students see their classmates?
4 What do they do at school camps?
5 Why does Becky like the *School of the Air*?
6 Which lessons are difficult for her?

**3** Find words in the text to match the definitions.

1 A place with fields and animals. [paragraph 2]
2 Near you. [paragraph 2]
3 Great, very nice. [paragraph 4]
4 Scientific tests. [paragraph 4]

**4** Would you like to be a *School of the Air* student? Why?/Why not?

# Grammar
## Present continuous (interrogative)

| Interrogative | | Short answers |
|---|---|---|
| Am I | | |
| Are you | | Yes, I am. |
| Is he she it | learning ... ? | No, they aren't. |
| Are we you they | | |

**5** Complete the questions about the picture and answer them. Use short answers.

Is Kylie **having** a radio lesson?
**Yes, she is.**

1 _____ her classmates _____ (sit) in the room?
2 _____ Kylie _____ (drink) orange juice?
3 _____ she _____ (work)?
4 _____ Kylie's dad _____ (talk) on the radio?
5 _____ her dad _____ (wear) jeans?

**6** Write questions.
1 what/you do?
2 you/study/English now?
3 where/you/sit?
4 what/your teacher/do/now?
5 what/you wear/today?
6 your father/work/now?

**7** Answer the questions in exercise 6.

# Vocabulary
## School subjects

**8** Complete the words with *a*, *e*, *i*, *o* and *u*.

g e o gr a phy

1 _ngl_sh    2 sc_ _nc_

3 c_mp_ter st_d_ _s    4 h_st_ry

5 _rts _nd cr_fts    6 sp_rt

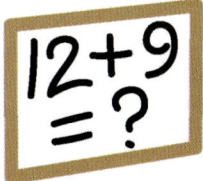 

7 m_ths    8 m_s_c

# Speaking

**9** Ask and answer with a partner.

What's your favourite subject?

Geography.

Why do you like it?

Because it's fun/interesting.

# Model text

**1** Read the text. Is your school day like Charlotte's or is it very different?

## My school day by Charlotte Wright

I really like school! I go to a very big school in Manchester, and my school day starts early. I get up at seven o'clock!

First, I cycle to school. I arrive at half past eight, but we start lessons at nine o'clock. My favourite subject is music. I'm learning to play the guitar.

We have lunch in the school canteen at twelve o'clock. The food isn't very nice! After that, we play with our friends until one o'clock.

We have more lessons in the afternoon. Then I go home at four o'clock. At home I always do homework. I'm doing a big history project at the moment.

Finally, I go to bed at about ten o'clock. I'm usually very tired!

**2** Read the text again and correct the false sentences.

1 Charlotte lives in Oxford.
2 She goes to school by bus.
3 She doesn't like music lessons.
4 Charlotte likes the food at her school.
5 She goes home after lunch.
6 She doesn't work in the evenings.

# Listening

**3** Listen to Justin and Lisa. Who doesn't like school? ▭

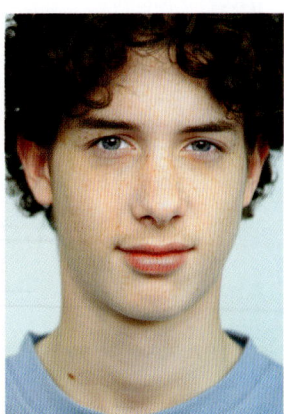

**4** Listen again and complete the sentences. ▭

Justin travels to school by **bus**.
1 His favourite subjects are _____ and _____.
2 He likes the _____ at school.
3 After school he usually plays _____.
4 Lisa's school is _____ minutes from her house.
5 She hasn't got a _____ subject.
6 Her school food is _____.
7 After school, she plays _____.

# Speaking

**5** Ask and answer with a partner.

> How do you go to school?

> What are your favourite subjects?

> What are you studying at the moment?

> What do you like about your school?

> What do you do after school?

# Writing

## first, then, after that and finally

We can use *first*, *then*, *after that* and *finally* to show the order of events.

| | | |
|---|---|---|
| first | = | the first event |
| then/after that | = | the next event |
| finally | = | the last event |

**6** Look again at the model text on page 54. Underline *first*, *then*, *after that* and *finally*.

**7** Choose the correct alternatives.

Helen always meets her friends at the weekend. At the moment she's waiting for them at home. Helen's friends always come to her house. **1** *First / Finally,* Helen's dad drives them in to town. **2** *Then / First*  they go shopping. They often buy some new CDs or books. **3** *After that / First,* they have lunch. They have a pizza or a hamburger. **4** *Finally / Then* after lunch, they often go to the park and play games. **5** *First / Finally,* they go to the cinema. They love comedy films.

**8** Write about your school day. Use the model text on page 54 and the writing guide to help you.

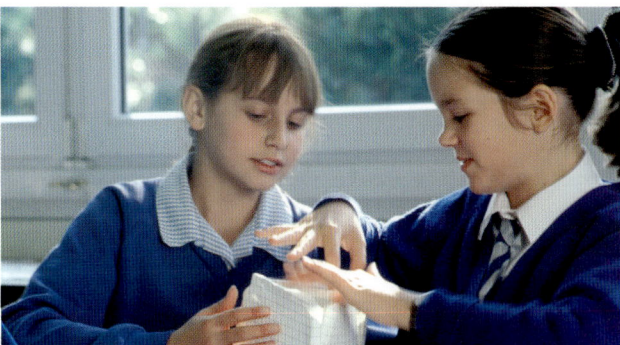

I go to school in...
First...
I... to school/I go to school by...
We start lessons at...
Then...
We have lunch at...
After that...
Finally...

# Song

**9** Listen and complete the song. Use the words in the box. 📼

> history   looking   things   play   teacher   maths

## My school

We're sitting in the classroom
The ¹ _____'s coming in
We're getting out our ² _____ books
Come on! Let's begin!

We're sitting in the classroom
We're ³ _____ at the board
We're learning about ⁴ _____
And we're working really hard

We're sitting in the classroom
We're putting ⁵ _____ away
We're waiting for the last bell
Great! Let's go and ⁶ _____!

1492
1963

**10** Answer the questions.

1 Where's the singer?
2 What lesson is it in Verse 1?
3 What lesson is it in Verse 2?
4 What does the singer want to do in Verse 3?

**11** Find words in the song to match the definitions.

1 Children have lessons here. (verse 1)
2 Start. (verse 1)
3 Teachers write on this. (verse 2)
4 This makes a loud noise. (verse 3)

# 8 Places

**1  Sam and Kate are in Megan's cave.**

Sam  Wow! This is a really strange place.
Kate  Look! There's a light.

**2  They find Megan.**

Megan  Hello. Who are you?
Kate  I'm Kate, and this is Sam. We're King Max's friends.
Sam  We want to find Imelda. D_ you know where she is?
Megan  I can look for her in my magic hologram.

**3  They see Imelda in the hologram.**

Megan  Look at the magic hologram ...
Sam  There's Imelda. She's building a machine.
Megan  She wants to destroy Max's submarine.
Kate  We must stop her, but where is she?
Megan  She's in her secret place. It's in a volcano.

**4  Megan gives them a present.**

Kate  We must go to the volcano and stop Imelda.
Megan  You can travel through the hologram. Take this magic flute. It can help you.
Sam  Wow! A magic flute! I love music.
Megan  Now step into the hologram and travel t_ the volcano.

**5  They travel through the magic hologram.**

Sam  Bye, Megan!
Kate  Come on, Sam.

---

**1** Are the sentences true or false? Correct the false sentences.

1  Megan has got a magic hologram.
2  She lives in a volcano.
3  Imelda wants to destroy Megan.
4  Megan gives Sam a musical instrument.
5  Sam and Kate travel to Max's submarine.

**2** Find words in the story to match the pictures.

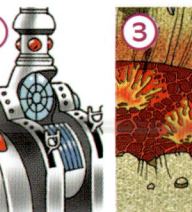

# Grammar

## Present simple and present continuous

> ### Present simple
> We use the present simple for habits, and things that are always true.
>
> *I love music.*          *I always get up early.*
>
> ### Present continuous
> We use the present continuous for actions that are happening now.
>
> *We're looking for Imelda.*     *It's raining at the moment.*
>
> > We don't usually use the present continuous with these verbs:
> > *be   have got   know   want   think*

**3** **Choose the correct alternatives.**

1 Sam and Kate *talk / are talking* to Megan.
2 Sam and Kate *look / are looking* for Imelda now.
3 Megan often *sees / is seeing* the future in her hologram.
4 Imelda *builds / is building* a machine at the moment.
5 Sam *loves / is loving* music.

**4** **Complete the text. Use the present simple or the present continuous.**

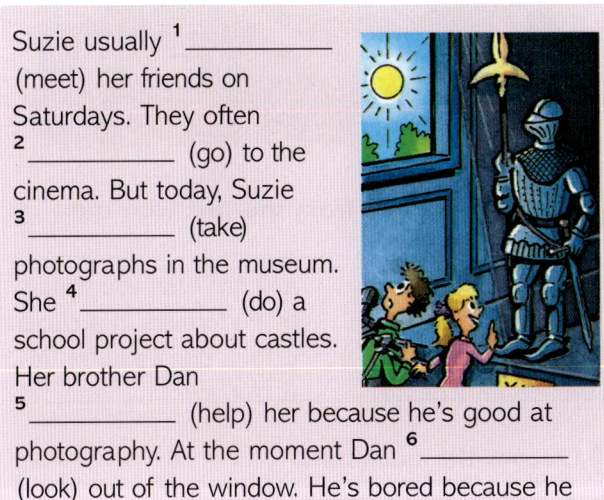

Suzie usually ¹_____ (meet) her friends on Saturdays. They often ²_____ (go) to the cinema. But today, Suzie ³_____ (take) photographs in the museum. She ⁴_____ (do) a school project about castles. Her brother Dan ⁵_____ (help) her because he's good at photography. At the moment Dan ⁶_____ (look) out of the window. He's bored because he ⁷_____ (not like) museums!

# Vocabulary

## Places to visit

**5** **Match the pictures with the words in the box.**

> museum   castle   park   zoo   cinema   beach

# Listening

**6** **Listen and identify the places from exercise 5.**

| | | | |
|---|---|---|---|
| 1 | **a** cinema | **b** | castle |
| 2 | **a** museum | **b** | park |
| 3 | **a** zoo | **b** | beach |
| 4 | **a** castle | **b** | museum |
| 5 | **a** beach | **b** | park |

# Speaking

**7** **Ask and answer with a partner.**

> What do you usually do at the weekend?

> What are you doing now?

> What clothes do you usually wear at the weekend?

> What are you wearing today?

# Writing

**8** **Write answers to the questions in exercise 7.**

# Reading

**1** **Read the text about a theme park. What things can you do there?** 📼

**1** go on rides ☐   **3** watch films ☐   **5** see animals ☐
**2** eat and drink ☐   **4** swim ☐   **6** buy things ☐

## Adventure World

**Adventure World is opening in Bromford next week. It's a new theme park for children.** *Leisure Weekly* **magazine talks to Tim Hicks, the park manager.**

**LW**   *Adventure World* is opening next week. What's
5       happening on the first day, Tim?

**Tim**   Well ... we're giving free tickets to children.

**LW**   That sounds great. Is food and drink free, too?

**Tim**   No, we aren't giving free food to visitors. But
        there are two shops, a café and a restaurant in
10      the park.

**LW**   Tell us more about the park.

**Tim**   Well, there are a lot of exciting rides. *Atlas* is one
        of my favourites. It's a roller coaster and it's very
        fast! There's also a ghost ride. It's called *Haunted*
15      *Castle*. It's very scary! Another great ride is *The*
        *Big Wave*. It's a water ride, and it's huge!

**LW**   Great! Are there any special events on the first
        day?

**Tim**   Yes. We're having a fireworks display in the
20      evening. A group of Chinese acrobats is
        performing, too. A rock band is playing in a
        special concert after that.

**LW**   What band is it?

**Tim**   That's a secret. Come to our opening day and
25      find out!

**2** **Read the text again and choose the correct answers.**

**1** On the first day, the park is giving free …
   **a** food.   **b** tickets.   **c** drinks.

**2** At the park there are a lot of …
   **a** cafés.   **b** rides.   **c** shops.

**3** *Haunted Castle* is very …
   **a** fast.   **b** big.   **c** scary.

**4** *The Big Wave* is a …
   **a** water ride.
   **b** roller coaster.
   **c** ghost ride.

**5** Tim's secret is about the …
   **a** circus performers.
   **b** fireworks display.
   **c** band.

**3** **Match the words from the text with the definitions.**

**1** free (line 6)          **a** I can't tell you this.
**2** display (line 19)      **b** Performers in a circus.
**3** acrobats (line 20)     **c** You don't pay for this.
**4** secret (line 24)       **d** A show.

**4** **Discuss the questions.**

**1** Would you like to visit *Adventure World*?
   Why/Why not?
**2** Which ride would you like to try? Why?

# Grammar

## Present continuous (future)

We can use the present continuous to talk about future arrangements.

*Adventure World **is opening** next week.*
*We **aren't giving** free food to visitors.*
*What**'s happening** on the first day, Tim?*

Future time expressions are usually at the end of a sentence.
*We're having a fireworks display **in the evening**.*

| | | |
|---|---|---|
| tonight | next week | this evening |
| tomorrow | on Monday | at the weekend |

**5** **Complete the sentences. Use the present continuous.**

1 I _____ (go) to the cinema on Tuesday.
2 We _____ (meet) Tanya in a café at twelve o'clock.
3 What _____ you _____ (do) next weekend?
4 My aunt and uncle _____ (visit) us next week.
5 _____ you _____ (watch) the match at the stadium or on TV?

**6** **Look at Sally's diary for the week and write sentences. Use the present continuous.**

*She's tidying her room on Monday.*

| | | |
|---|---|---|
| | Mon | tidy room |
| 1 | Tues | go shopping |
| 2 | Wed | finish a school project |
| 3 | Thu | play basketball |
| 4 | Fri | watch film at cinema with Nikki |
| 5 | Sat | do my homework |
| 6 | Sun | visit Aunt Mary |

# Vocabulary

## Places in a town

**7** **Write the correct words.**

café   post office   library   clothes shop
kiosk   swimming pool   theatre   bank

# Listening

**8** **Listen to Sarah and James talking on the telephone. Why do they want to meet?** 📼

**9** **Listen again and complete Sarah's diary.** 📼

**Saturday**

| | |
|---|---|
| Morning | going [1] _____ |
| Lunch | making a [2] _____ |
| Afternoon | having a [3] _____ |
| Dinner | going to an [4] _____ |
| Evening | watching [5] _____ |

# Speaking

**10** **Ask and answer about your plans. Ask about** *this evening*, *tomorrow* **and** *next weekend*.

What are you doing this evening?

I'm visiting …

# Model text

**1** **Read Amy's letter. Where is her penfriend from?**

Althorpe Drive
Birmingham
23 February

Dear Anna

How are you? I'm really looking forward to your visit! We're meeting you at the airport on Friday night.

On Saturday, my parents are taking us to London. We're visiting the Tower of London. Then we're taking a boat trip on the river. You can take some great photos! In the afternoon, we're going to the theatre. There's a children's play called *Beauty and the Beast*. It's fantastic! After the play, my dad wants to take us to a Chinese restaurant. Are there any Chinese restaurants in Paris?

I haven't got any plans for Sunday and next week! What do you want to do? I can't wait to see you!

Best wishes

Amy

**2** **Read the letter again and correct the false sentences.**

1  Amy lives in London.
2  Anna is coming to Britain by boat.
3  She's arriving on Saturday.
4  Amy and Anna are visiting the Tower of London on Sunday.
5  They're going to the cinema on Saturday afternoon.
6  They're having dinner at home on Saturday night.
7  Anna is leaving on Sunday.

# Listening

**3** **Listen to the interview. How many people does the man talk to?**

**4** **Listen again and answer the questions.**

1  Which country is Renata from?
2  What does she like in London?
3  What is she doing this afternoon?
4  Where are Fernando and Carlos from?
5  Which museum are they visiting this afternoon?
6  What's Carlos' favourite place?

# Speaking

**5** **Ask and answer with a partner.**

> Are there any nice places in your town?

> Where do tourists visit?

> Is there any special food in your town?

> Why do you like ...?

# Writing

## Informal letters

When you write an informal letter to a friend …

- write your address at the top on the right.
- write the date under the address.
- start the letter with *Dear* + your friend's name.
- finish the letter with *Best wishes* or *Love* + your name.

**6** Put the letter in the correct order. Use Amy's letter on page 60 to help you.

**a** ☐ 19 August

**b** ☐ Thanks for your letter. How are you? What are you doing? I'm really enjoying school this year.

**c** ☐ Please write soon.
Best wishes
Tom

**d** ☐ I'm in the school football team this year. I train a lot and I also play a lot of matches. We're playing a match in Scotland next week.

**e** ☐ 41, Marsdon Terrace Manchester

**f** ☐ Dear Jacob

**7** Imagine your pen friend is visiting you next week. Write a letter and tell him/her your plans. Use the model text and the writing guide to help you.

Dear ...
I'm really looking forward to...
On Saturday/Sunday we're ...
In the morning/afternoon, ...
I can't wait to see you.
Best wishes

# Song

**8** Listen and complete the song. Use the words in the box. 📼

> next   come   excited   meeting   arriving   zoo

## My penfriend

My penfriend's coming
We're $^1$_____ him tonight
He's travelling by plane
He's on the $^2$_____ flight

He's $^3$_____ at the airport
At a quarter past two
I'm really $^4$_____
I'm planning things to do

We're going to the funfair
And maybe to the $^5$_____
We're visiting a castle
Why don't you $^6$_____, too?

**9** Complete the puzzle with words from the song. What's the extra word?

1 A very old building.
2 Planes arrive here.
3 You fly in this.
4 You write to this person.
5 The opposite of *go*.
6 There are a lot of rides here.

## Vocabulary

### School subjects

**1** Match the sentences with the words in the box.

> history    geography    science
> computer studies    English    sport
> maths    music    arts and crafts

'This is a great website!'  *computer studies*

1 'I'm learning to play the piano.'
2 'Open your geometry books at page 32.'
3 'I know a lot of words, but I'm not good at grammar.'
4 'What's the capital of Poland?'
5 'We've got athletics training today!'
6 'Lucy's picture is really nice.'
7 'In 1492, Christopher Columbus …'
8 'Hydrogen and oxygen make water.'

### Places to visit

**2** Match the places with the words in the box.

> beach  castle  cinema  museum  park  zoo

## Places in a town

**3** Complete the words with *a*, *e*, *i*, *o* and *u*.

1  b_nk

2  sw_mm_ng p_ _ l

3  th_ _ tr_

4  l_br_ry

5  cl_th_s sh_p

6  p_st _ff_c_

7  c_f_

8  k_ _ sk

## Vocabulary extra

**4** Choose the correct answers.

1  I'm tired. Let's sit down on this _____.
   **a** cave  **b** bench  **c** palace
2  My cousin lives on a _____. Her parents have got a lot of animals.
   **a** park  **b** farm  **c** stadium
3  I can walk to my _____ sports centre.
   **a** local  **b** wise  **c** free
4  Sarah is really good at music. She can play the _____.
   **a** machine  **b** hologram  **c** flute
5  Sorry, I can't tell you. It's a _____ .
   **a** ride  **b** subject  **c** secret

# Grammar

## Present continuous (affirmative and negative)

**5** Look at the picture and complete the affirmative and negative sentences.

1  The students in Class A _____ (have) a sports lesson today.
2  They _____ (train) for a basketball match.
3  The sport's teacher _____ (smile).
4  Player number 5 _____ (run).
5  He _____ (tie) his shoelaces.
6  Numbers 8 and 13 _____ (play) at the moment.
7  They _____ (sit) on a bench.

## Present continuous (interrogative)

**6** Write the questions to complete the dialogues.

| Anna | Mum and Dad/watch TV? |
|------|------------------------|
|      | 1 _____ . |
| Tim  | Yes, they are.         |
| Anna | they/watch a film?     |
|      | 2 _____ . |
| Tim  | No, they aren't. They're watching a football match. |

| Sally | you/do your homework? |
|-------|------------------------|
|       | 3 _____ . |
| Mila  | Yes, I am.             |
| Sally | What/you study?        |
|       | 4 _____ . |
| Mila  | History.               |
| Sally | you/revise for the test? |
|       | 5 _____ . |
| Mila  | Yes, I am.             |

## Present simple and present continuous

**7** Write sentences. Use the present simple or the present continuous.

> Our teacher/never/shout at us
> *Our teacher never shouts at us.*
>
> The students/do/a test now
> *The students are doing a test now.*

1  My mum/usually/take/me to school
2  At the moment/we/study/English
3  Lucy/play/basketball in the school team
4  I/not do/homework at the moment
5  I/hate/the food at school
6  It/not rain today

## Present continuous (future)

**8** Complete the text with the words in the box.

> go (x2)  do  have  meet  watch  visit

I ¹_____ a lot of things next weekend. On Saturday I ²_____ my friend Jack in the town. I ³_____ lunch with Jack's family in a pizza restaurant! On Saturday evening I ⁴_____ to the cinema with my family. We ⁵_____ a great film about gangsters.

On Sunday morning my grandma ⁶_____ us. Then in the afternoon, I ⁷_____ to my best friend's birthday party!

# 9 Music

**1** Sam and Kate arrive at the volcano.

Sam This is the volcano. And there's Imelda's mobile palace.
Kate Look. There's a platform, but how can we go down to it?
Sam Hey! We can use that metal ladder.
Kate OK. Let's go!

**2** They climb into the volcano.

Sam It's very hot in here. I'm scared!
Kate Don't worry, Sam. Look! Here's a tunnel.

**3** They see Imelda's guards.

Sam That ladder was terrible. Were you scared?
Kate No, I wasn't! Come on!
Sam Wait! Two guards are coming down the tunnel.
Kate What shall we do?
Sam Let's play the magic flute.
Kate Good idea, Sam.

**4** The guards fall asleep.

Kate The guards are sleeping. Well done, Sam.

**5** They see Imelda's secret place.

Sam Wow! Look at this place! Look at all those amazing machines.
Kate There's Imelda. We must stop her. How can we take the crystal?
Sam I don't know. We need a plan.

**1** Put the events in order.

1 Sam plays the flute. ☐
2 They see Imelda's guards. ☐
3 They climb down the ladder. ☐
4 Sam and Kate arrive at the volcano. ☐
5 The guards go to sleep. ☐

**2** Find words in the story to match the definitions.

1 You climb this. [picture 1]
2 A long, underground place. [picture 2]
3 Horrible. [picture 3]
4 You do this at night. [picture 4]
5 An idea. [picture 5]

# Grammar

## past simple: *be*

| Affirmative | Negative | Interrogative |
|---|---|---|
| I was | I was not/wasn't | Was I …? |
| you were | you were not/weren't | Were you …? |
| he she it was | he she it was not/wasn't | Was he she …? it |
| we you they were | we you they were not/weren't | Were we you …? they |

| Short answers | there was/there were |
|---|---|
| Yes, I was. No, we weren't. | *There was* a great concert last week. *There weren't* many tickets. |

**3** Correct the false sentences.

Mike was at the cinema yesterday.

Mike wasn't at the cinema yesterday. He was at a concert.

**1** Ella and Lisa were at a football match last Tuesday.

**2** Jenny was at school yesterday.

**3** Tim and Alex were in the park last Friday.

**4** Simon was at home yesterday.

**5** Sarah was at a rock concert last weekend.

**4** Complete the dialogue.

**Billy** ¹_____ you at home yesterday evening?
**Dan** No, I ²_____. I ³_____ at my cousin's birthday party.
**Billy** ⁴_____ it a good party?
**Dan** Yes, it ⁵_____.
**Billy** ⁶_____ the music good?
**Dan** No, it ⁷_____. But there ⁸_____ some great food!

# Listening

**5** Look at the advert for a pop quiz programme. What do the competitors do?

> Listen to **Pop Quiz** and guess the mystery pop stars!
>
> Tonight 8p.m. on **Radio Beat**
>
> **109.5 FM**

**6** Listen to the programme and complete the table. 📼

## Pop Quiz

| | pop singer 1 | pop singer 2 |
|---|---|---|
| man or woman? | woman | ⁴_____ |
| hair colour | ¹_____ | dark |
| nationality | ²_____ | ⁵_____ |
| pop singer's name! | ³_____ | ⁶_____ |

# Speaking

**7** Play *Pop Quiz*. Student A thinks of a singer and Student B guesses who it is.

> This singer is from Britain and he's got black hair.

> Is it Robbie Williams?

> Yes, that's right!

# Reading

**1** **Look at the pictures and the title. Is the text about …**

**a** a TV show?

**b** a music competition?

**c** a concert?

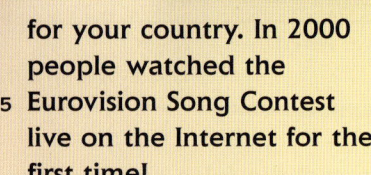

# Eurovision

**Do you watch the Eurovision Song Contest on TV? This week *Music World* magazine looks at the history of the event.**

Every year millions of people watch the Eurovision Song Contest on TV. In fact, it's probably the most
5 popular music competition in the world. But it was very small when it started. In 1956, singers from seven countries travelled to
10 Lugano, in Switzerland for

the first Eurovision song contest. Today twenty-four countries compete in the contest, and people in
15 many more countries watch it on TV.

In the past, the competitors used their own language, but today singers can
20 choose their language. Most competitors now sing in English, so you can sing all the songs, too.

In the past, judges from
25 each country voted for the songs in the competition. But in 1998 telephone voting started. Now TV audiences can phone and
30 vote for their favourite songs. You can vote for any singer, but you can't vote

for your country. In 2000 people watched the
35 Eurovision Song Contest live on the Internet for the first time!

2004 was another important year for
40 Eurovision. A Junior Eurovision Song Contest started. The first contest was in Copenhagen, Denmark. Children from
45 eighteen countries performed, and the young singers were amazing! The winner of the first contest in Denmark was Dino, from
50 Croatia. He has got a fantastic voice and the audience loved his song. Now he's a pop star! Perhaps Junior Eurovision
55 can make you a star, too?

**2** **Read the text and check your answers to exercise 1.** 📼

**3** **Read the text again and answer the questions.**

1 When was the first contest?
2 How many countries compete in the Eurovision Song Contest today?
3 What language do most singers use?
4 What happened in 1998?
5 Why was 2004 an important year?
6 Who was the first junior winner?

**4** **Match the words from the text with the correct definitions.**

| | | | |
|---|---|---|---|
| 1 | contest (line 3) | **a** | You sing or talk with this. |
| 2 | judges (line 24) | **b** | Give points. |
| 3 | audience (line 29) | **c** | People who choose the winners. |
| 4 | vote (line 30) | **d** | Competition. |
| 5 | voice (line 51) | **e** | People at a show. |

**5** **Discuss the questions.**

1 Do you watch the Eurovision Song Contest?
2 Would you like to compete in a song contest?

# Grammar

## Past simple: regular verbs (affirmative)

| perform | performed | clap | clapped |
|---------|-----------|------|---------|
| play | played | plan | planned |
| dance | danced | try | tried |

**6** Complete the sentences. Use the past simple affirmative.

1  David _____ (play) the guitar at the school concert yesterday.
2  The rain _____ (stop) after half an hour.
3  Jess _____ (invite) us to her party.
4  I _____ (study) very hard for the test.
5  We _____ (smile) for the photo.
6  The film _____ (finish) at nine o'clock.

**7** Complete the text with the verbs in the box. Use the past simple affirmative.

> dance   like   help   clap   practise   call   try

My cousin Anne was a competitor in a national junior song contest. Two other girls ¹_____ on stage with her. They ²_____ a lot before the contest and they were really good. The audience ³_____ Anne's song very much and they ⁴_____ a lot. Her father is a musician and he ⁵_____ her to write the music. She ⁶_____ her song 'Sweet Dreams'. Anne ⁷_____ very hard, but she wasn't the winner.

# Vocabulary

## Musical instruments

**8** Complete the words with *a, e, i, o* and *u*.

h a rm o n i c a     1  s_x_ph_n_

2  dr_ms     3  p__n_

4  v__l_n     5  k_yb__rds

6  tr_mp_t     7  _l_ctr_c g__t_r

# Listening

**9** Listen and write the correct musical instrument from exercise 8.

1  _____     4  _____
2  _____     5  _____
3  _____     6  _____

# Speaking

**10** Student A mimes an instrument. Student B guesses their partner's instrument.

What instrument is this?

No, that's wrong!

Yes, that's right!

It's a trumpet.

Is it a saxophone?

# Model text

**1** **Read the text. Why does Alice like Beyoncé?**

My favourite singer by Alice Jones

Beyoncé is my favourite singer, and she's really beautiful. She's from Texas, in the USA. She can't play a musical instrument, but she sings and dances really well.

Beyoncé started singing when she was a child. Later, she was a singer in the pop band Destiny's Child. Their first two albums were fantastic. Then Beyoncé decided to be a solo singer.

My favourite Beyoncé song is 'Crazy in Love'. It's a brilliant love song. I like Beyoncé because her music is really good. You can sing and dance to all her songs.

**2** **Read the text again. Are the sentences true or false? Correct the false sentences.**

1 Beyoncé is British.
2 She's very pretty.
3 She plays the keyboards.
4 Beyoncé started singing when she was young.
5 She was in a rap band.
6 The band's first two albums were terrible.
7 Now Beyoncé is a solo singer.

# Listening

**3** **Listen to music reporters Liz and Des. Whose concert was good?** 🔲

**4** **Listen again and complete the reporters' notes.** 🔲

## The Skinks

When? 1 _____.
The fans weren't happy because the 2 _____ arrived late.
The Skinks only played for 3 _____.
Their songs were 4 _____.

Liz

## Amber Jade

When? 5 _____.
Amber Jade's music was 6 _____.
Amber Jade can play the 7 _____.
The fans 8 _____ all night.

Des

# Speaking

**5** **Ask and answer with a partner.**

Do you play a musical instrument?

Which instrument do you play?

What type of music do you like?

Do you listen to music in your language or in English?

Who are your favourite singers and bands?

What's your favourite song?

# Writing
## Checking your spelling

When you finish your writing, check your spelling carefully. Use a dictionary.

**6** Underline and correct the spelling mistakes.

My freind loves dancing.

*My friend loves dancing.*

1 Sory, I don't know that pop singer's name.
2 There's a good disco near the beech.
3 The consert finished at eleven o'clock.
4 Can you play the gitar?
5 It's an intresting book about Eminem.
6 I think rock music is terribel.

**7** Write about your favourite singer. Use the fact file or your own ideas and the writing guide. Check your spelling!

FACT FILE

| name | Britney Spears |
|---|---|
| from | USA |
| musical instruments | none |
| history | in TV adverts when she was eight |
| first album | Baby One More Time (1999) |
| best song | Toxic |

... is my favourite singer.
He's/She's from ...
He/She can/can't ...
He/She started ... when he/she was ...
His/Her first album ...
My favourite song is ...

# Song

**8** Listen and choose the correct alternatives.

## Music in the park

Do you remember last **¹night / week**?
We were in the park
We **²danced / played** in a cool band
Until it was dark

You played the **³guitar / piano**
I played the drum
Jimmy played the **⁴trumpet / saxophone**
It was really good fun

The crowd **⁵liked / loved** the music
They danced in the **⁶rain / sun**
They clapped at the end
Let's do it again!

**9** Answer the questions.

1 Where were the singer and his friends last night?
2 What were their musical instruments?
3 What was the weather like?

**10** Look at the song again. Which words rhyme with these words?

park **dark**
drum ¹_____
rain ²_____

# 10 TV

**1** **Imelda explains her plan.**

**Imelda** The machine is finished.
**Kate** Oh no! We must stop her, but how?
**Sam** Ssh. I'm thinking!
**Imelda** With this machine I can destroy Max's submarine forever. Ha! Ha! Nero! Put the crystal into the machine.
**Nero** Yes, Queen Imelda.

**2** **Nero puts the crystal into the machine.**

**Kate** What can we do?
**Sam** What about our magic hat? When Tess wore it, she became invisible.
**Kate** You're right. Give it to me.

**3** **Kate wears the magic hat.**

**Sam** Kate! Where are you? I can't see you.
**Kate** I'm here. Now I can steal the crystal. Wait for me here!

**4** **Kate takes the crystal.**

**Imelda** The machine is ready. Nero! Destroy Max's submarine!
**Nero** Yes, Queen Imelda. Hey! Nothing happened. The machine is broken!
**Imelda** Where's the crystal? Somebody took it!
**Nero** Hey! Look at the TV screens. It's that boy again! He stole it!
**Imelda** Catch him!

**5** **Sam and Kate run away.**

**Sam** Well done, Kate. We've got the crystal!
**Kate** Yes, but the guards saw you. Come on, Sam. Let's go!

**1** **Correct the false sentences.** 📼

1 Imelda wants to destroy the machine.
2 Kate has an idea.
3 Sam puts on the hat.
4 Nero sees Kate on the TV screen.
5 Nero catches Sam and Kate.

**2** **Match the words from the story with the definitions.**

1 forever (picture 1)     a You can use it now.
2 steal (picture 3)     b It doesn't work.
3 broken (picture 3)     c A very long time.
4 ready (picture 4)     d Take.

# Grammar

## Past simple: irregular verbs

> ### Past simple: irregular verbs
>
> Some verbs are irregular in the **past**.
>
> | do | did | come | came | go | went |
> |---|---|---|---|---|---|
> | get up | got up | have | had | steal | stole |
> | meet | met | leave | left | wear | wore |
>
> ### Time expressions
>
> | yesterday | in 1999 | last week |
> |---|---|---|
> | yesterday afternoon | two days ago | last month |

**3** Complete the sentences about the story. Use the list of irregular verbs on page 107.

1 Sam and Kate _____ (hide) behind a box.
2 Sam _____ (have) an idea.
3 Kate _____ (wear) the magic hat.
4 She _____ (steal) the crystal.
5 Nero _____ (see) Sam.
6 Sam and Kate _____ (run) away.

**4** Complete Sarah's e-mail. Use the past simple and the verbs in the box.

do   have   make   go   meet   be   get up

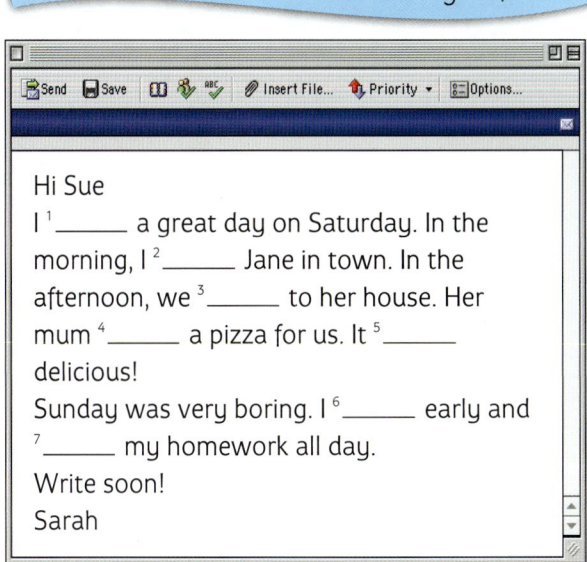

Hi Sue
I ¹_____ a great day on Saturday. In the morning, I ²_____ Jane in town. In the afternoon, we ³_____ to her house. Her mum ⁴_____ a pizza for us. It ⁵_____ delicious!
Sunday was very boring. I ⁶_____ early and ⁷_____ my homework all day.
Write soon!
Sarah

# Vocabulary

## Adjectives

**5** Match the pictures with the words in the box.

boring   exciting   interesting
funny   sad   frightening

# Listening

**6** Listen to Lisa and Billy. What TV programmes do they like? 📼

 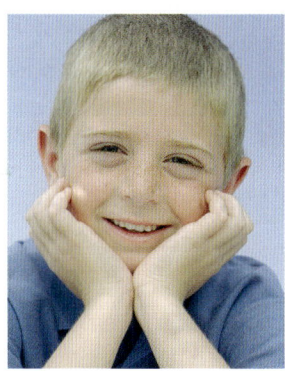

**7** Listen again. Are the sentences true or false? 📼

1 Lisa met her sister outside the school.
2 She went to a gymnastics class last night.
3 She watched a film.
4 Billy did his homework last night.
5 He watched two cowboy films.
6 The second film was funny.

# Speaking

**8** Tell your classmates what you did last night.

> I went to the cinema with my parents.

# Reading

**1** **Look at the photos. Do you watch TV programmes about animals? Why?/Why not?**

TV Review magazine

## *In The Wild* - a children's TV documentary.

Last month *In The Wild* filmed six children at an orang-utan centre in Borneo. What did they do? Eleven-year-old Tracy Andrews told us about the trip.

'I flew to Borneo with five other children and the camera crew. Then we travelled by boat to the centre.'

'The centre looks after sick baby orang-utans and studies them. The orang-utans stay in cages at first and then they learn to live in the jungle. Naturalists sit on wooden platforms in the jungle and watch the orang-utans. We built a new platform for the centre, and the camera crew filmed us.'

'We lived in tents in the jungle, and it was quite scary! One boy didn't like snakes, and the cameraman was scared of spiders. On my first night, I was frightened, too. I listened to the birds and animals all around me, and I didn't sleep for ages!'

'After ten days, we finished the new platform in the jungle. It was a great experience. I was sad sometimes because I missed my family, but I had a lot of fun, too. I can't wait to watch the programme on TV!'

**2** **Read the text. What did the children build?** 📼

**3** **Read the text again and choose the correct answers.**

1 The children went to Borneo …
  a last year.
  b last month.
  c six weeks ago.
2 Tracy travelled to the centre by …
  a train and boat.
  b plane and car.
  c plane and boat.
3 At first, the orang-utans live …
  a in the jungle.
  b on platforms.
  c in cages.
4 The cameraman was scared of …
  a spiders.
  b orang-utans.
  c snakes.
5 Tracy was sometimes sad because …
  a she didn't like her work.
  b she didn't like the other children.
  c she wanted to see her family.

**4** **Find words in the text to match the pictures.**

**5** **Would you like to visit this place? Why?/Why not?**

# Grammar

## Past simple (negative, interrogative and short answers)

**Negative** *didn't* + verb.
One boy **didn't like** spiders.

**Interrogative** *did* + subject + verb
What **did they do?**   Where **did they go?**

**Short answers**
Yes, they did.       No, they didn't.

**6** Look at the pictures and correct the sentences.

Ian listened to music last night.
**Ian didn't listen to music last night. He watched TV.**

**1** Susie wrote an e-mail on Saturday.

**2** Mark ate a hamburger for lunch.

**3** Lisa and Dorota played tennis yesterday.

**4** Sarah bought a book on Friday.

**5** Vicky and Pete went to London last week.

**7** Write the questions.

what/you/do/last weekend?
**What did you do last weekend?**
you/go/to the beach/last summer?
**Did you go to the beach last summer?**

**1** you/do/your homework last night?
**2** what/you/have/for breakfast?
**3** you/go/to the cinema last month?
**4** what time/you/get up/this morning?
**5** you/read/a magazine yesterday?

**8** Answer the questions from exercise 7.

# Vocabulary

## TV programmes

**9** Match the pictures with the words in the box.

> sport   cartoon   soap opera   documentary
> film   comedy   quiz show   the news

# Speaking

**10** Ask and answer with a partner.

> Did you watch TV last night?

> What programme did you watch?

> What kind of TV programmes do you like?

# Model text

**1** **Read the text. Why does Mike like *Hill School*?**

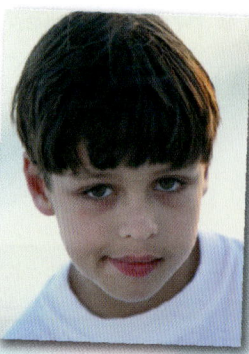

*My favourite TV programme*

*By Mike Matthews*

My favourite programme is a soap opera. It's called Hill School. It's on TV three times a week, and it's about a school in Manchester. I really like the characters. **They**'re very interesting and they're just like people in my school in Bristol. Hill School is fantastic. These are my favourite episodes.

Last month, Charlie and his sister Sally started at the school. They're new characters in the programme. At first, everybody at Hill School really liked **them**. Sally was funny and Charlie was really good at football. Then, in last week's episode, Charlie stole a Walkman from John Watts. And **he** lied to **him** about it! Later Sally cheated in **her** maths exam. After that, everybody at the school thought they were horrible.

Hill School is a really good soap opera because it's very exciting. I can't wait to see what happens next!

**2** **Read the text again and answer the questions.**

1 What type of programme is *Hill School*?
2 How many times a week is it on TV?
3 Where is Mike's school?
4 Who are the new characters in the programme?
5 Who stole John's Walkman?
6 What did Sally do?

# Listening

**3** **Listen to a survey about TV programmes. What programmes do the children mention?** 📼

soap operas ☐
sport ☐
comedy programmes ☐
films ☐
quiz shows ☐
the news ☐
documentaries ☐

**4** **Listen again and complete the sentences.** 📼

Robert is **ten** years old.
1 He likes soap operas and _____.
2 *Team Champions* is a _____ show.
3 The show always has two _____.
4 Mary thinks it's very _____.
5 John watches documentaries about _____.
6 He also likes _____.

# Speaking

**5** **Ask and answer with a partner.**

**What's your favourite programme on TV?**

**What kind of programme is it?**

**Why do you like it?**

**What's your favourite episode?**

# Writing

## Reference words

**6** Look again at the text on page 74 and match the reference words with their meanings.

| | | | |
|---|---|---|---|
| **1** | It | **a** | John Watts |
| **2** | they | **b** | the soap opera |
| **3** | them | **c** | Sally |
| **4** | he | **d** | the soap opera characters |
| **5** | him | **e** | Charlie and Sally |
| **6** | her | **f** | Charlie |

**7** Change the red words to reference words.

Paul is watching a film. The film is boring.
*Paul is watching a film. It's boring.*

1 Toby is my favourite character. Toby is really funny.
2 Harry watches films on Harry's new DVD player.
3 I like quiz shows. Quiz shows are great fun.
4 Mary likes documentaries. Mary's favourite documentaries are about animals.
5 Lisa and Ben are new characters. Lisa and Ben's mum is a teacher at the school.

**8** Write about your favourite TV programme. Use the model text and the writing guide to help you.

My favourite TV programme is …
It's on TV … times a week.
It's about …
The characters are …
Last month …
In last week's episode …
It's really … because

## Song

**9** Listen and complete the song. Use the words in the box. 📼

funny   comedy   telephoned   end   TV

### The TV star

I sat down last night
And turned on the ¹_____
And there was Jenny Jones
Starring in a ²_____
The film was very ³_____
And I laughed until the ⁴_____
And then I turned it off
And I ⁵_____ my friends

Jenny Jones, Jenny Jones
Do you remember her?
She was at our school last year
Now she's a TV star! (x2)

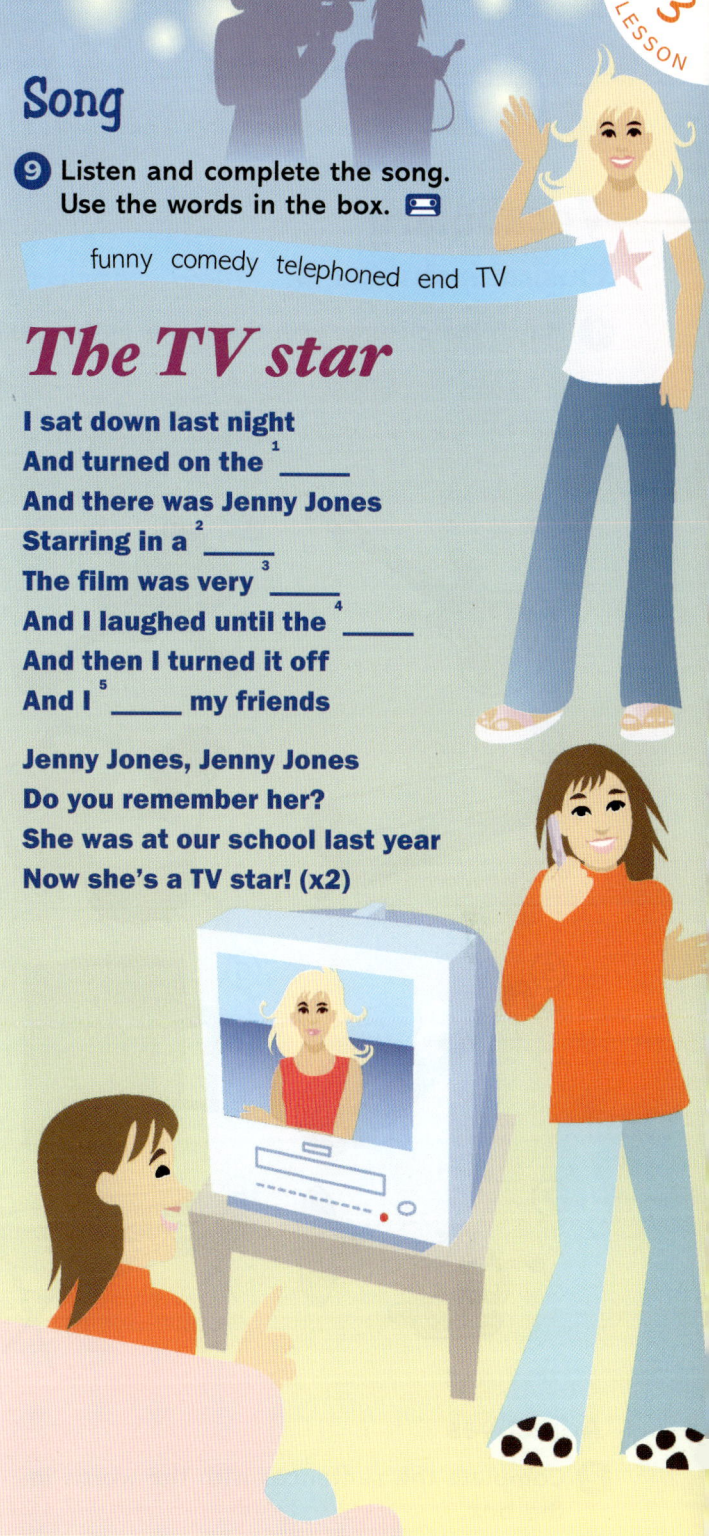

**10** Answer the questions.

1 Where did the singer see Jenny Jones?
2 Who did the singer telephone?
3 Where did the singer first meet Jenny?
4 What job does Jenny do now?

**11** Find the past simple forms in the song.

| sit | **sat** |
|---|---|
| turn | ¹_____ |
| laugh | ²_____ |
| telephone | ³_____ |
| is | ⁴_____ |

## Vocabulary

### Musical instruments

**1** Match the pictures with the words in the box.

> drums  saxophone  keyboards  piano
> electric guitar  violin  trumpet  harmonica

① ② ③ ④ ⑤ ⑥ ⑦ ⑧

## TV programmes

**3** Read the sentences and complete the crossword.

### Across

**3** *Grass Valley* is a _____ about the lives of children in California. I watch it every night.

**5** I love _____ programmes. Especially football matches.

**6** I saw *Troy* last night. It's a great _____!

**8** Did you watch_____? The president of China visited New York.

### Down

**1** Let's watch a _____ about Africa.

**2** There's a _____ on TV. It's The Flintstones!

**4** *Money Race* is an exciting _____. Every week one person wins a million Euros!

**7** I watched a really funny _____ programme last night.

## Adjectives

**2** Complete the sentences with the words in the box.

> boring  exciting  frightening
> funny  interesting  sad

**1** Lucy told me a really _____ story yesterday. I laughed a lot.

**2** We watched an _____ documentary about elephants. I love documentaries.

**3** Saturday was a really _____ day. It rained all day, and I didn't go out.

**4** I don't like horror films because they're really _____.

**5** The book was really _____. I cried a lot.

**6** It was a very _____ football match. Our team scored a goal in the last minute!

## Vocabulary extra

**4** Complete the words with *a, e, i, o* or *u*.

**1** l_dd_r

**3** t_nn_l

**5** _ _d_ _ nc_

**2** scr_ _n

**4** j_ngl_

**6** _r_ ng- _t_n

# Grammar

## Past simple: be

**5** Complete the e-mail with the correct past simple form of *be*.

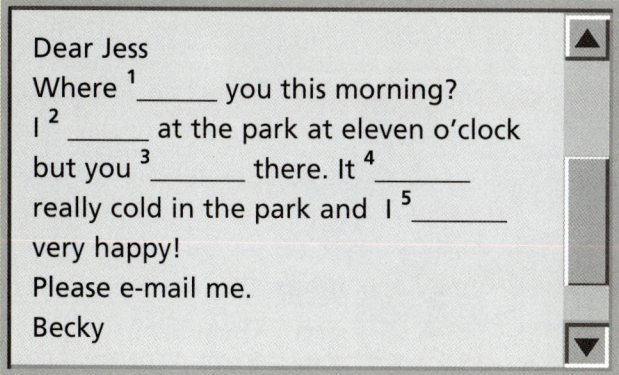

Dear Jess
Where ¹_____ you this morning?
I ²_____ at the park at eleven o'clock
but you ³_____ there. It ⁴_____
really cold in the park and I ⁵_____
very happy!
Please e-mail me.
Becky

## Past simple: regular verbs (affirmative)

**6** Write sentences about the pictures. Use the verbs in the box.

plan  play  dance  tidy  watch

1 Josh _____ at a party.

2 Lucy _____ basketball.

3 Jason _____ his bedroom.

4 Vicky _____ a film on TV.

5 Sally and Ann _____ their summer holiday.

## Past simple: irregular verbs

**7** Complete the text with the correct form of the verbs.

We ¹_____ (go) to Lindsay's party last Saturday and we ²_____ (have) a great time! I ³_____ (wear) my new jeans and everybody liked them. The food was really good, too. Lindsay's mum ⁴_____ (make) some really nice cakes. I ⁵_____ (eat) a lot! We danced and ⁶_____ (sing) songs at the party, too. The music was great! I ⁷_____ (leave) the party at nine o'clock. On Sunday morning, I ⁸_____ (get up) really late!

## Past simple (negative, interrogative and short answers)

**8** Complete the dialogue.

| Sally | *Did you watch* (you/watch) the new Spiderman film at the weekend? |
|---|---|
| Mark | No, I didn't. |
| Sally | It wasn't very good. I ¹_____ (not like) _____ it. |
| Mark | What ²_____ (you/do) on Sunday? ³_____ (you/go) to the beach? |
| Sally | No, we ⁴_____ . The weather was horrible. |
| Mark | ⁵_____ (your parents/take) you to the new swimming pool? |
| Sally | No, they ⁶_____ . |
| Mark | That's terrible! |

# 11 Clothes

**1** Sam and Kate climb out of the volcano.

Sam  Hurry up! The guards are coming.
Kate  I can't. Look at my shirt. Help me!
Sam  Take my hand!

**2** They run through the desert.

Sam  Quick! This way!
Kate  It's OK. We're faster than the guards.
Sam  But Imelda and Nero have got sand bikes. Look!

**3** Sam hurts his foot.

Sam  Ow! My foot!
Kate  Come on! Get up, Sam!
Sam  I can't.
Kate  Yes, you can. We must run. We can't fight them, Sam! They're stronger than us.
Sam  But my foot hurts.
Kate  Take off your shoe. Come on!

**4** They can't escape.

Sam  My foot's worse than before. I must sit down.
Kate  No, Sam. We must go back to Max.
Sam  But I can't walk. Hey! Remember Tess's magic seeds.
Kate  But what are they for?
Sam  I don't know. Maybe they can help us. Let's find out.

**5** A magic forest appears.

Sam  Wow! It's a forest. It came from the magic seeds!
Kate  Well done, Sam.
Sam  Let's go back to the submarine.
Kate  Magic ring! Take us to Max!

**1** Answer the questions.

1 Who can't climb up the ladder at first?
2 What have Imelda and Nero got?
3 Why can't Sam run?
4 What does he remember?
5 What happens when he throws the seeds?

**2** Find words in the story to match the definitions.

1 Be quick! (picture 1)
2 A dry place. (picture 2)
3 Stand up! (picture 3)
4 Discover. (picture 4)

# Grammar

## Comparative adjectives

**Short adjectives**

long ➞ longer          big ➞ bigger
nice ➞ nicer           pretty ➞ prettier

**Long adjectives**

fashionable ➞ **more** fashionable
expensive ➞ **more** expensive

**Irregular adjectives**

good ➞ better
bad ➞ worse
far ➞ further

We use *than* to compare two things or people.
*Beth is **prettier than** her sister*
*My bike is **better than** yours.*

**3** Complete the sentences with comparative adjectives and *than*.

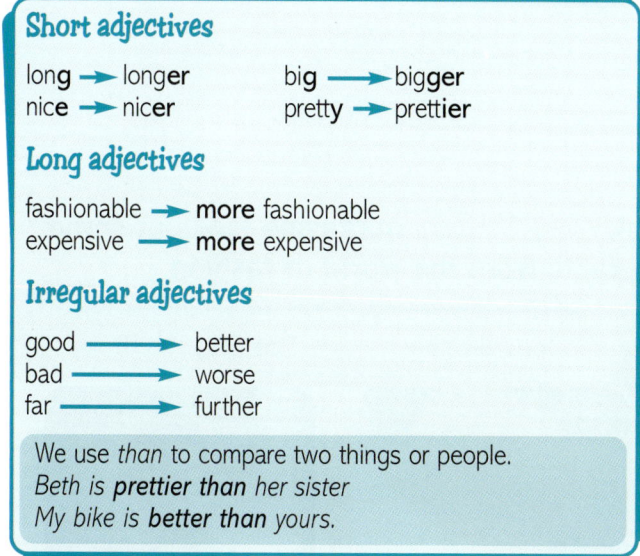

1 Kate is _____ (brave) Sam.
2 The sand bikes are _____ (fast) Sam and Kate.
3 Sam is _____ (intelligent) Nero.
4 The volcano is _____ (hot) the desert.
5 The guards are _____ (strong) Sam and Kate.
6 Max is _____ (nice) Imelda.

**4** Write sentences.

   Tim's bag/big/Sarah's bag
   **Tim's bag is bigger than Sarah's bag.**

1 Your shoes/clean/my shoes
2 Their house/far/our house
3 Sean's T-shirt/nice/David's shirt
4 Ronaldo/famous/David Beckham
5 My jacket/fashionable/Emma's jacket

# Vocabulary

## Accessories

**5** Match the pictures with the words in the box.

backpack  belt  cap  gloves  scarf  sunglasses

# Listening

**6** Look at the picture. Listen to two people in a clothes shop and tick the things they buy. 📼

# Speaking

**7** Ask and answer with a partner about the picture in exercise 6. Use the adjectives in the box.

pretty  warm  big  expensive  fashionable  long

Are the pink gloves warmer than the black gloves?

No, they aren't.

# Reading

**1** Look at the photos. What clothes and accessories can you see?

**2** Read the text and answer the questions.

1 Which piece of clothing is the biggest?

2 Which piece of clothing is the oldest?

## Crazy Clothing

**This week *Cool Clothes* magazine looks at some amazing facts from the world of fashion.**

**The most expensive jeans**

**The tastiest clothes**

**The longest scarf**

**The biggest shoes**

**A** How much did your jeans cost? The world's most expensive jeans cost an amazing €38,139! They're valuable because they're the world's oldest jeans: in fact, they're 120 years old! The Levi Strauss company bought them in 2001 for their old jeans collection.

**B** The clothes in this photo look like normal clothes, but you can eat them! Each year there's a special 'chocolate fashion show' in New York. Famous fashion designers and chefs make clothes from chocolate. They look great, but you can't wear them outside in the sun!

**C** The world's longest scarf was 43.4 kilometres long. That's the distance of a marathon race! Groups of women all over the world made parts of the scarf from wool. It took them three years! Later they cut the scarf into 2,500 wool blankets, and gave the blankets to poor people.

**D** Matthew McGray is 2.3 m tall and he weighs 280 kg. He's a very big man, and he's got the biggest feet in the world! He wears huge size 69 shoes! He pays a lot of money for special leather shoes because he can't buy his shoes in a shop.

**Do you know any amazing fashion records? Contact us at *Cool Clothes* magazine!**

**3** Read the text again. Are the sentences true or false? Correct the false sentences.

1 The world's most expensive jeans cost €38.

2 In 2001 the Levi Strauss company bought a pair of old jeans.

3 You can wear chocolate clothes in hot weather.

4 A lot of women made the world's longest scarf.

5 You can see the world's longest scarf today in a museum.

6 Matthew McGray is very short.

7 His shoes are very expensive.

**4** Match the words from the text with the definitions.

1 valuable (paragraph A)

2 chef (paragraph B)

3 blanket (paragraph C)

4 leather (paragrah D)

a You put this on a bed.

b This person makes food.

c Expensive.

d A material.

**5** Which record is the most interesting? Why?

# Grammar

## Superlatives

### Short adjectives

| | | |
|---|---|---|
| long | ⟶ | the longest |
| nice | ⟶ | the nicest |
| big | ⟶ | the biggest |
| pretty | ⟶ | the prettiest |

### Long adjectives

| | | |
|---|---|---|
| exciting | ⟶ | the most exciting |
| expensive | ⟶ | the most expensive |

### Irregular adjectives

| | | |
|---|---|---|
| good | ⟶ | the best |
| bad | ⟶ | the worst |
| far | ⟶ | the furthest |

**6** Look at the picture and write sentences. Use superlative adjectives.

be/tall/girl
**Kelly is the tallest girl.**
wear/fashionable/jeans
**Jane is wearing the most fashionable jeans.**

1 have got/expensive/watch
2 have got/long hair
3 wear/old/T-shirt
4 be/short/girl
5 carry/big/backpack
6 wear/comfortable/shoes

# Vocabulary

## Clothes

**7** Complete the words with *a*, *e*, *i*, *o* and *u*.

1 dr__ss

2 sh_rt

3 sk_rt

4 sw__tsh_rt

5 tr__ners

6 T-sh_rt

7 sw__t_r

8 sh__s

9 tr__s_rs

10 j_ck_t

# Speaking

**8** Ask and answer with a partner about the students in your class. Use the adjectives in the box.

big   fashionable   smart   old   nice   pretty

**Who has got the nicest shoes?**

# Writing

**9** Write five sentences about students in your class. Use your ideas from exercise 8.

# Model text

**1** **Read the text. Who is the most fashionable person in Jane's family?**

### My family and fashion
by Jane Watson.

This is a photo of my sister Nina. My sister loves fashion! She reads fashion magazines every week and she spends a lot of money on new clothes. In fact, she's the most fashionable person in my family. She usually wears pretty dresses or short skirts and great T-shirts. But I can't borrow her clothes because she's five years older than me.

I really like fashion. I sometimes go to clothes shops with my sister. My favourite clothes are trainers. I've got a lot of them, and my friends wear them all the time. I like designer clothes, too. But I can't buy them often because they're very expensive!

My mum and dad aren't really interested in fashion. My mum likes comfortable clothes, and she usually wears jeans and a sweatshirt. My dad wears smart trousers and shirts at work, but he usually wears his oldest clothes at home.

**2** **Read the text again and answer the questions.**

1 Why can't Jane borrow her sister's clothes?
2 What does Jane do with her sister?
3 Why doesn't she buy many designer clothes?
4 Who aren't interested in fashion?
5 When does her dad wear smart clothes?

# Listening

**3** **Listen to the children. Why are they unhappy?** 📼

**4** **Listen again and write the correct names from the box.** 📼

> Ellie   Billy   Tina   Jack

Who had a birthday party last week?   **Ellie**
1 Who won something in a school competition?   _____
2 Who bought a skirt?   _____
3 Who doesn't like a new jacket?   _____
4 Who received a present from an aunt?   _____
5 Who normally goes shopping with his mother?   _____
6 Who wants to go to the beach?   _____

# Speaking

**5** **Ask and answer the clothing questionnaire with a partner.**

### Clothing Questionnaire:
#### How fashionable are you?

1 What are your favourite clothes?
2 What clothes do you hate?
3 What colours do you like?
4 Who buys your clothes?
5 How often do you go shopping for clothes?
6 Do you read fashion magazines?

# Writing

## Order of adjectives

We can use colours and other adjectives in descriptions. The colour adjective usually comes after the other adjective.

*I usually wear my **old white** trainers.*
*She's got a **big blue** backpack.*

**6** **Put the words in the correct order.**

She wore pretty jacket a blue
**She wore a pretty blue jacket.**

1 I've got shoes a pair of white small
2 It's big a grey bag
3 He's got black shoes old
4 That's expensive an yellow hat
5 She new a bought red bag
6 I'm wearing comfortable sweatshirt blue a

**7** **Write about your family and fashion. Use the model text and the writing guide to help you.**

... is the most fashionable person in our family
My favourite clothes are ...
My ... usually wears ...
... is/isn't interested in fashion

# Song

**8** **Listen and complete the song. Use the words in the box.** 📼

cooler  trousers  skirt  scarf  expensive  jeans

## Suzy's clothes

My clothes are smarter than Suzy's
I wear ¹_____ and dresses and hats
But she looks better in an old red sweater
Blue ²_____ and a baseball cap

My clothes are ³_____ than Suzy's
I buy them in Tokyo
But she looks better in an old red sweater
A ⁴_____ and a yellow bow

My clothes are more ⁵_____
I go to the very best shops
But she looks better in an old red sweater
A ⁶_____ and a pair of socks

**9** **Find ten clothes and accessories in the song.**

*trousers*

**10** **Find the comparative forms in the song.**

smart        ¹_____
good         ²_____
cool         ³_____
expensive    ⁴_____

# 12 Holidays

**1 Sam and Kate return to the submarine.**

| | |
|---|---|
| Max | You're back! |
| Sam | Yes. And we've got the crystal! |
| Max | That's wonderful! |
| Sam | Here's your magic ring, and here's your hat. |
| Tess | Thanks. |

**2 Max tells them about his plans.**

| | |
|---|---|
| Max | Thank you, my friends. Now I can return to Crystalia. |
| Kate | What are you going to do now? |
| Max | I'm going to catch Imelda. Then I'm going to travel round Crystalia. |

**3 Imelda is outside.**

| | |
|---|---|
| Sam | There's Imelda! |
| Kate | How did she find us here? |
| Sam | She's going to open the door! |
| Kate | She's going to take the crystal! |
| Max | I can catch her in my net. |

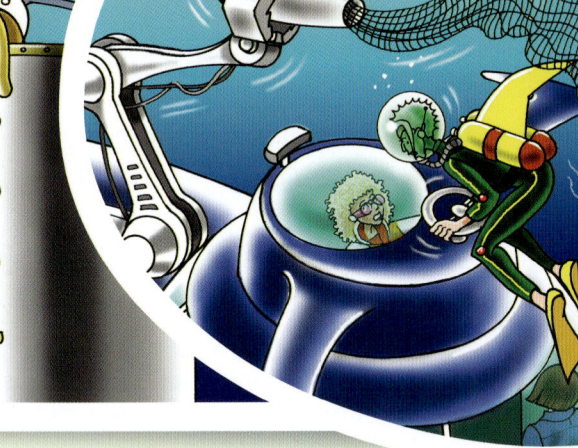

**4 Max and Tess say 'Goodbye'.**

| | |
|---|---|
| Kate | Are you going to put Imelda in prison? |
| Max | Yes, I am. Goodbye and thank you. We aren't going to forget you. |
| Kate | Goodbye, Max. Goodbye Tess. |
| Sam | Bye Tess. Bye Max. |

**5 They go home.**

| | |
|---|---|
| Kate | Look. It's going to rain. It's always sunny in Crystalia. |
| Sam | That's true. But I never want to see Imelda or Nero again. |
| Kate | Well ... They're far away now. Come on! Let's go home. |

**1 Are the sentences true or false? Correct the false sentences.**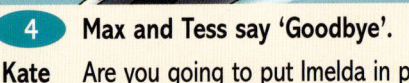

1 The children bring the crystal to Max.
2 Max wants to travel round Britain.
3 Imelda tries to steal the crystal.
4 Sam and Kate catch Imelda in a net.
5 The children go to Crystalia.

**2 Match the words from the story with the definitions.**

1 wonderful (picture 1)
2 net (picture 3)
3 prison (picture 4)
4 Far away (picture 5)

a Not near.
b You catch fish with this.
c Great.
d A place for criminals.

# Grammar

## going to

> We use *going to* to talk about future plans and intentions.
>
> I'm **going to** catch Imelda.
> We **aren't going to** forget you.
> Are you **going to** put Imelda in prison?

**3** Complete the sentences. Use the affirmative or negative form of *going to*.

1 Max _____ have a holiday.
2 He _____ put Imelda in prison.
3 The people of Crystalia _____ have a party.
4 Tess and Max _____ forget Sam and Kate.
5 Sam and Kate _____ walk home.

**4** Write the questions in the dialogue. Use *going to*.

**Toby** what/you/do/in the holidays
**What are you going to do in the holidays?**

**Harry** I'm going to go to the beach with my family.

**Toby** ¹you/swim/in the sea?

**Harry** Yes, I am.

**Toby** ²you/play beach volleyball?

**Harry** No, I'm not. I don't like volleyball.

**Toby** ³where/you/stay?

**Harry** At my grandparents' house. They live by the sea.

**Toby** ⁴How/you/travel there?

**Harry** We're going to go there by car.

**Toby** ⁵you/do any homework in the holidays?

**Harry** No. I'm going to have a rest!

# Vocabulary

## Holidays

**5** Match the pictures with the words in the box.

> safari   cruise   beach holiday
> skiing holiday   camping holiday

# Listening

**6** Listen to the radio interview. Are the sentences true or false?

> **What are you going to do in the school holidays?**
>
> Listen to **Holidays** for some great holiday ideas
>
> **Radio 5   8p.m.**

1 Mark is going to visit Africa.
2 He's going to go to the beach.
3 Hannah is going to visit her penfriend.
4 She's going to go diving.
5 Alex is going to visit a lot of museums.

# Speaking

**7** Ask and answer with a partner about your holiday plans. Use the ideas in the box.

> get up early   go to the beach   travel
> visit your relatives   play sport

> Are you going to get up early?

## Reading

**1** **Look at the pictures. What topics do you think the text mentions?**

holiday activities ☐   food ☐   ways to travel ☐   weather ☐   hobbies ☐   places to stay ☐

**2** **Read the text and check your answers to exercise 1.** 🔲

# Holidays in the future.

**What will holidays be like in the year 2050? Will they be very different? We asked four young people to make predictions.**

**A** I think there will be a hotel on the moon and people will travel there by rocket. Inside the hotel it'll be sunny and warm all the time, and tourists will play sport or relax. People will also go outside in space suits and explore the moon's surface. I'd love to go to a place like that!
**Simon, 12**

**B** In the future, new computer programs will give us virtual holidays! We won't get on a plane and fly because we won't *really* travel. We'll sit in a machine, and the computer will take us to different virtual places in the world. We'll visit Rome or New York, but we won't move from our seats.
**Tanya, 11**

**C** There will be very fast jet planes in the future. We'll fly to Australia in an hour, or to Russia in minutes. We'll visit some ancient ruins for lunch, and lie on a tropical beach in the afternoon. Transport will be cheap and easy. I can't wait!
**David, 14**

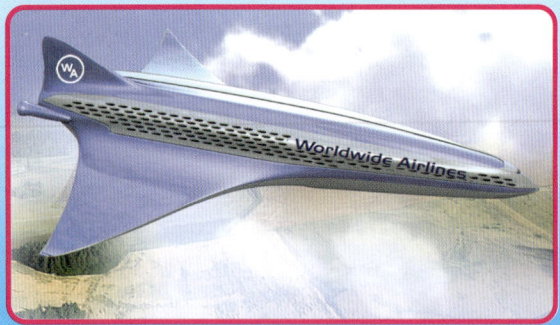

**D** The climate will be different in the future. It will be very, very hot and so we won't go to the beach for our holidays. Everybody will go to huge indoor holiday resorts. Inside, there will be artificial beaches and an artificial sea. There will even be artificial snow for skiing.
**Megan, 10**

**3** **Read the text again and write the correct names.**

Megan   Simon   David   Tanya

Who thinks it will be much hotter?   **Megan**
**1** Who thinks we won't travel?   _____
**2** Who talks about holidays on the moon?   _____
**3** Who talks about a winter sport?   _____
**4** Who says planes will be faster?   _____
**5** Who talks about computer holidays?   _____

**4** **Find words in the text to match the definitions.**

**1** You wear these in space. (paragraph A)
**2** Not real. (paragraph B)
**3** Very old. (paragraph C)
**4** Normal weather. (paragraph D)
**5** Not natural. (paragraph D)

**5** **Which predictions do you agree with? Why?**

# Grammar

## will (predictions)

We use *will* to make predictions about the future.

It **will**/It'**ll** be sunny and warm all the time.
We **won't** move from our seats.
What **will** holidays be like in the year 2050?
**Will** they be very different?
Yes, they **will**.   No, they **won't**.

**6** Complete the predictions. Use *will* or *won't* and your own opinions.

1 Robots _____ teach children in schools.
2 In the future, people _____ live on the moon.
3 The weather _____ be warmer.
4 Astronauts _____ find life on the planet Mars.
5 Everybody _____ speak the same language.
6 Children _____ have pet aliens.

**7** Write the questions.

America/send astronauts to Venus?
**Will America send astronauts to Venus?**

Who/win/the next World Cup?
**Who will win the next World Cup?**

1 you/go/to university?
2 where/the Olympics/be/in 2016?
3 you/be/famous?
4 Gwen Stefani/make/a new album next year?
5 the weather/be/nice in November?

**8** Ask and answer the questions in exercise 7.

# Vocabulary

## The weather

**9** Match the pictures with the words in the box.

> It's foggy.   It's windy.   It's sunny.
> It's raining.   It's snowing.   It's cloudy.

①    ②

③    ④

⑤   ⑥

# Listening

**10** Listen and write five of the words from exercise 9.

1 _____   4 _____
2 _____   5 _____
3 _____

# Speaking

**11** Ask and answer with a partner.

> What's the weather like today?

> What's the weather usually like in December?

> What's your favourite time of year?

## Model text

**1** Read the text. Would you like to visit Sun City? Why?/Why not?

# Come to Sun City!

What are you going to do this summer? Why not come to Sun City, in South Africa?

The weather in Sun City is very hot, and the sun always shines! In fact, you can sunbathe on New Year's day!

You'll have a great time at your luxury hotel in Sun City. You can play sport, go to the disco or relax in the swimming pool. You'll love the food, too. Try a 'braie'. It's a delicious South African barbecue!

You can do a lot of exciting things in Sun City. Visit the water park for a really exciting day! It's near to the hotel, and it's great fun!

In Sun City you can go on a safari, too. Sun City is near to the Pilansberg Safari Park. You'll see elephants and lions in the park, so bring your camera!

**You'll have a great time in Sun City!**

**2** Read the text again and answer the questions.

1  Where is Sun City?
2  What's the weather like in Sun City?
3  What can you do in the hotel?
4  What special food can you eat?
5  What animals can you see at the safari park?

## Listening

**3** Listen to the *Dream Holiday Quiz*. Who wins the prize? 📼

**4** Listen again and complete the sentences. 📼

The quiz contestants can win a holiday for their **family**.

1  *Walt Disney World* is in _____.
2  You can see _____ in India.
3  The pyramids are _____ years old.
4  The island of Santorini is a _____.
5  Lucy wants to go to _____.

## Speaking

**5** Imagine you win the *Dream Holiday Quiz*. Ask and answer the questions.

> Where are you going to choose for your dream holiday?

> Who are you going to go with?

> What are you going to do?

> What will the weather be like?

## Writing

### Checking for mistakes

When you finish writing, always check your work for mistakes. Look for …

- spelling mistakes.
- punctuation mistakes.
- grammar mistakes.

**6** Underline the mistakes in the sentences and correct them.

I'm going to learn Italian <u>becuse</u> I want to visit Italy. *because*

1 I think it rains tomorrow.
2 I never go shopping when Im' on holiday.
3 We're going stay at home this year.
4 My dad have got a new digital camera.
5 The wether will be great in July.
6 We went to France last year:

**7** Write an advert for a dream holiday. Use the model text on page 88 and the writing guide to help you.

Come to …
Why not …
The weather in … is …
Stay at …
You can …
Try a …
You'll see …

## Song

**8** Listen and choose the correct alternatives.

# Holiday time

We're going to have a [1] **party**/**holiday**
We're going to stay by the sea
We're going to [2] **walk**/**drive** there tomorrow
My family and me

The weather [3] **won't**/**will** be cloudy or cold
It'll be sunny and fine
We're going to [4] **wear**/**take** our summer clothes
We're going to have a good time

We're going to [5] **sit**/**run** on the beach
We're going to swim in the sea
We're going to [6] **buy**/**eat** some ice cream
My family and me

**9** Complete the puzzle with words from the song. What's the extra word?

1 Good weather.
2 You can find sand here.
3 Your mum, dad, brothers and sisters.
4 You can eat this. It's cold!
5 The season after spring.
6 You do this in the sea.

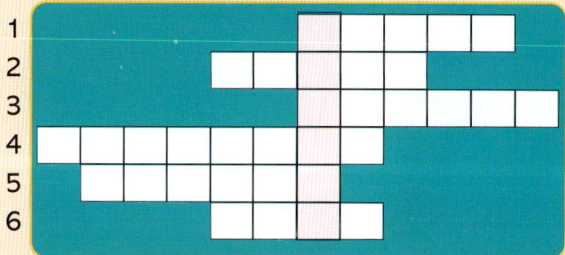

## Vocabulary

### Accessories

**1** Match the sentences with the words in the box.

> backpack  belt  cap  gloves  scarf  sunglasses

1 You wear this on your head.
2 You wear these in sunny weather.
3 You wear this round your neck.
4 You put books and other things in this.
5 You wear these on your hands in cold weather.
6 You wear this with jeans or trousers.

### Clothes

**2** Match the clothes in the picture with the words in the box.

> dress  jacket  shirt  skirt  sweater  sweatshirt  T-shirt  shoes  trainers  trousers

### Types of holiday

**3** Complete the sentences with the words in the box.

> beach holiday  camping holiday  cruise  safari  skiing holiday

1 I saw an elephant when I was on a _____ in Kenya.
2 My friend went on a fantastic _____ round the Pacific Ocean.
3 My family loves swimming so we always go on a _____ .
4 I had a great _____ . There was a lot of snow in the mountains.
5 I don't want to go on a _____ . I want to stay in a hotel!

### The weather

**4** Write sentences about the places on the map.

*It's snowing in Chicago.*

¹ Chicago
² New York
³ Washington
⁴ Atlanta
⁵ New Orleans
⁶ Miami

## Vocabulary extra

**5** Circle the odd word out.

1 sea  blanket  desert  island
2 chef  designer  teacher  prison
3 rich  valuable  money  fact
4 wonderful  amazing  explore  fantastic
5 old  new  ancient  artificial
6 climate  weather  virtual  rain

# Grammar

## Comparative adjectives

**6** Look at the picture and write sentences.

Bryan/be/strong/Lenny

*Bryan is stronger than Lenny.*

1 Joe/be/intelligent/Lenny
2 Bryan/be/tall/Lenny
3 Bryan/sunglasses/be/big/Joe's
4 Lenny's/clothes/be/interesting/Bryan's
5 Joe's/hair/be/short/Lenny's hair

## Superlatives

**7** Complete the questions with superlative adjectives. Then choose the correct answers.

1 Which is _____ (big) country in the world?
  a France  b Italy  c Russia

2 Which country has got _____ (nice) beaches for swimming?
  a Iceland  b Turkey  c Austria

3 Which is _____ (good) country for safari holidays?
  a Kenya  b France  c Egypt

4 What is _____ (cold) place in the world?
  a Germany  b Antartica  c Scotland

5 Which country is _____ (close) to the Mediterranean?
  a Egypt  b Thailand  c Ireland

## going to (plans)

**8** Complete the text with the affirmative or negative of *going to*.

*I'm not going to* go to school tomorrow because it's Saturday. I'm really tired so I ¹_____ get up early.
My brother Dan ²_____ go shopping because he ³_____ buy a present for his girlfriend.
In the afternoon, Dad ⁴_____ play football with Dan in the park, but I ⁵_____ go with them because I ⁶_____ help my mum at home.

Dan loves music, and on Sunday he ⁷_____ play the guitar all day. But I've got an exam on Monday so I ⁸_____ do my homework!

## will (predictions)

**9** Choose the correct alternatives.

1 The weather *will* / *won't* be very hot in the summer holidays.

2 My football team *will* / *won't* win a lot of matches because they aren't very good.

3 Perhaps my grandparents *will* / *won't* visit us today. It's my dad's birthday.

4 My sister is good at maths. Maybe she *will* / *won't* help me with my homework.

5 It *will* / *won't* rain very much in August.

6 I'm going to Tim's party tonight. It *will* / *won't* be great!

# Project 1

## Reading

**1** Read Sarah's poster. What are her friends' names?

### All about me!

My name's Sarah and I'm ten years old. I'm from Liverpool, in Britain. It's a great city!

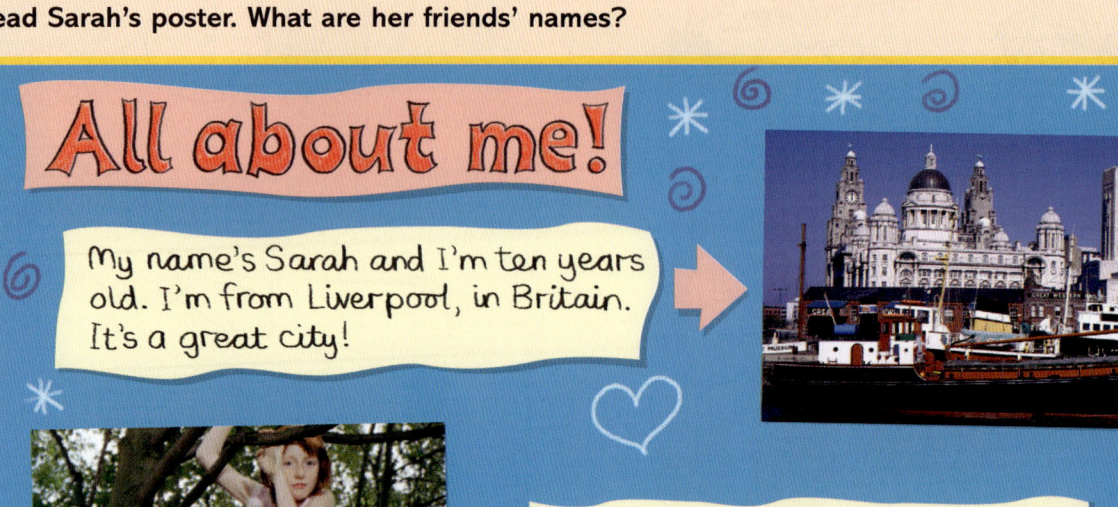

This is me with my best friend, Lisa. We're classmates. Lisa has got black hair. She's really funny!

My neighbours Hannah and Tom are good friends, too. Hannah is ten. She's tall and she's got long hair. Her brother Tom is twelve. He's really nice.

My favourite sports are swimming and diving. I'm in the school swimming team.

My favourite food is Pizza, but I like hamburgers, too.

I love Eminem. His concerts are fantastic!

This is my dog Pepper. He's crazy!

**2** Look at the poster on page 92 and complete the notes.

| Name | Sarah |
|---|---|
| age | ten |
| nationality | 1 _____ |
| best friend | 2 _____ |
| neighbours | 3 _____ and 4 _____ |
| favourite sports | 5 _____ and 6 _____ |
| favourite food | 7 _____ |
| favourite pop star | 8 _____ |
| pet | 9 _____ |

# Vocabulary

**3** Match the pictures with the words in the box.

city   tall   hamburger   diving   concert   hair

**4** Match the definitions with the words from exercise 3.

1 This is a sport.
2 You see pop stars here.
3 You can eat this.
4 This person isn't short.
5 This is on your head.
6 A lot of people live here.

# Speaking

**5** Ask and answer the questions.

Where are you from?

Who are your friends?

Who are your neighbours?

What's your favourite sport?

What's your favourite food?

Which pop stars or singers do you like?

Have you got a pet?

# Writing

**6** Complete the table about you.

| | |
|---|---|
| name | _____ |
| nationality | _____ |
| best friends | _____ |
| favourite sport | _____ |
| favourite food | _____ |
| favourite pop star or singer | _____ |
| pet or favourite animal | _____ |

**7** Write about you, and your favourite people and things. Then find or draw pictures to make a poster. Use the project guide to help you.

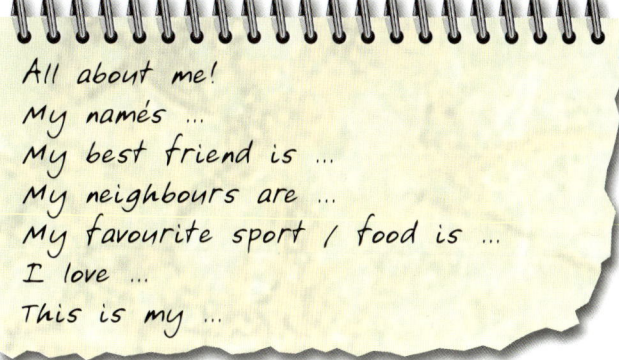

All about me!
My name's ...
My best friend is ...
My neighbours are ...
My favourite sport / food is ...
I love ...
This is my ...

**8** Display your poster in the classroom.

# Project 2

## Reading

**1** Read about Tom's family. How many brothers and sisters has he got?

Hi! I'm Tom, and this is my family.

# My Family

**Elizabeth**

My grandma is 60. She likes books and films.

**Jack**

My grandad is 67. He watches sport on TV.

**Sally** = **David**

This is my mum. She's a teacher.

This is my dad. He's a doctor.

**Michael** = **Helen**

My uncle works in a supermarket.

My aunt is an artist.

**Tom**

This is me! I'm 10. I love football.

**Anna**

My sister is 12. She plays the cello.

**Harry**

My brother is 5. He likes dinosaurs.

**Jessica**

This is our cousin. She's only 4 years old. She's got a lot of toys.

**2** **Look at the poster on page 94 and correct the sentences.**

Elizabeth is Jack's sister.
*Elizabeth is Jack's wife.*

1 Helen's dad plays sport.
2 Anna and Jessica are sisters.
3 Tom and Harry are cousins.
4 Elizabeth is Jessica's aunt.
5 Anna's aunt is a teacher.
6 Tom's sister likes sport.
7 Michael is Helen's brother.
8 Harry is Michael's son.

# Vocabulary

**3** **Find words in the poster to match the pictures.**

**4** **Match the definitions with the words from exercise 3.**

1 This is a musical instrument.
2 You can buy food here.
3 Young children play with these.
4 This person works in a hospital.
5 This person likes art.
6 These animals are very big.

# Speaking

**5** **Look again at the poster. Ask and answer questions with a partner.**

Who is ... ?

How old is ... ?

Who is Tom's ... ?

What job does ... do?

# Writing

**6** **Make a list of the people in your family and write notes about them.**

My brother    6 years old.
               He likes football.
Mum          40 years old.
               She's a teacher.

**7** **Write two or three sentences about each person in your family. Add photos or draw pictures to make a family tree poster. Use the project guide to help you.**

Hi. I'm ...
This is my family.
This is my ...
He/she ... likes/plays/works ...
My ... is a doctor/teacher.
... is ... years old.
He/she has got/likes ...

**8** **Display your poster in the classroom.**

## Reading

**1** Read the advertisement for a fantastic house. What can you do there?

| | | |
|---|---|---|
| watch films ☐ | go swimming ☐ | dance ☐ |
| play football ☐ | play computer games ☐ | go skiing ☐ |

### Come and stay in the 'Island House'

This amazing house is on the beautiful island of Vanunu, in the Pacific Ocean. Children can come here for a holiday. The house has got six bedrooms. There are computers, TVs and robots in every room. The robots do the housework and they cook your favourite food!

You can do a lot of things inside the house. There's an Internet room and a small cinema in the house. You can play computer games and watch all your favourite films! You can play table tennis and other games in the games room. And there's a disco room with a dance floor so you can have great parties!

Outside, there's a beautiful garden with palm trees, a big swimming pool and a tennis court. A lot of pretty birds live in the garden. The house is next to the beach! You can swim in the sea or go snorkelling and see the fish!

The Island House is a fantastic place.

**2** Look at the poster on page 96 and choose the correct answers.

1 The house is …
 a on an island.  b in a town.
 c on a mountain.
2 The house has got six …
 a TVs.  b bedrooms.  c swimming pools.
3 Cooking and cleaning are easy because the house has got …
 a robots.  b kitchens.  c computers.
4 In the garden there are a lot of …
 a fish.  b animals.  c birds.
5 You can play tennis
 a in the garden.  b on the beach.
 c in the games room.

# Vocabulary

**3** Complete the words from the poster with *a, e, i, o* and *u*.

_sl_nd

t_bl_ t_nn_s

tr_ _s

d_nc_ fl_ _ r

sn_rk_ll_ng

r_b_t

**4** Complete the sentences with the words from exercise 3.

1 My _____ is a very intelligent machine.
2 Let's play _____. It's my favourite game.
3 I love this song! Let's go to the _____.
4 I like _____ because I love fish.
5 There are a lot of _____ in the park.
6 Vanunu is an _____. There's water all around it.

# Speaking

**5** Ask and answer questions with a partner.

Where is your house?

How many bedrooms has it got?

What's your favourite room?

What's your bedroom like?

Has it got a balcony/a garden?

What can you do in your area?

# Writing

**6** Imagine your ideal house. Answer the questions and write notes.

1 Where is your ideal house?
2 What rooms has it got?
3 Has it got computers, robots or TVs?
4 What can you do in the house?
5 What sports or activities can you do?

**7** Write a description of your ideal house and add photos or draw pictures to make a poster. Use the project guide to help you.

Come and stay in …
This amazing house is…
The house has got …
There's a … inside the house.
Outside, there's a …
… is a fantastic place.

**8** Display your poster in the classroom.

# Project 4

**1** Look at Hazel's timetable. How many subjects are there?

## My ideal school timetable

### 9 a.m. Dance lessons
We learn different types of dancing at school. I like ballet and disco dancing. It's great fun!

### 10 a.m. Cookery
In cookery lessons we learn new recipes for cakes and sweets. Our teachers help us to cook them. My favourite food is chocolate cake.

### 11 a.m. English
For English lessons we read English magazines and listen to English songs. We often go to London and watch a play. English is fantastic!

### 12 o'clock. Lunch time
The teachers cook a barbecue for us every lunch time! We listen to music and eat great food!

### 1 p.m. Sport
I love sport. We do a lot of different sports at school. Sometimes we go to the beach and do windsurfing. We also play football and basketball.

### 2 p.m. Internet studies
We learn about our favourite stars on the Internet, and we play computer games! At the moment we're making our own websites, too.

**2** Look at the poster on page 98 and answer the questions.

1 What do students make in cookery lessons?
2 What do they do in London?
3 Who cooks the food at lunch time?
4 What do they do at the beach?
5 What are they doing in their Internet studies lesson at the moment?

# Vocabulary

**3** Match the words in the box with the pictures.

ballet recipe barbecue play windsurfing

**4** Match the definitions with the words from exercise 3.

1 This is a kind of dancing.
2 You watch this at a theatre.
3 You cook this outside.
4 You do this at the beach.
5 This tells you how to cook something.

# Speaking

**5** Play *Guess the mystery school subject.* Student A describes a school subject. Student B guesses the subject.

> In this lesson we learn about people in the past.

> History!

> Yes. That's right!

**6** Now change roles and do exercise 5 again.

# Writing

**7** Imagine your ideal school timetable. Answer the questions and write notes.

1 What are your ideal school subjects?
2 What do you do in each subject?
3 What do you do at lunch time?
4 What school trips do you have?

**8** Write about the subjects in your ideal timetable. Add photos or draw pictures to make a poster. Use the project guide to help you.

8 a.m. ... lesson
For ... lessons, we ...
I love ...
Sometimes we ...
In ... lessons we learn ...
At the moment ...

**9** Display your poster in the classroom.

# Project 5

## Reading

**1** Read the poster. Who are the music stars and where are they from?

### Super Music Stars

Robbie Williams is British. He's a fantastic singer and a great songwriter. He started his music career in a band called 'Take That'. The band was very successful, but Robbie decided to leave them because he wanted to be a solo singer. His first album as a solo singer was very successful. Today, millions of fans listen to his music. Two of his famous songs are 'Angels' and 'Millennium'. Robbie is a superstar!

Avril Lavigne is a fantastic singer. She writes songs and she plays the guitar! She's also really pretty! She was born in Ontario, Canada in 1984. She started to play the guitar and sing when she was only twelve years old. She became famous when she was only sixteen! Avril's song 'Complicated' is really popular.

Justin Timberlake is American. He's very good-looking and he's a great singer, too. Justin Timberlake was in the teenage pop band NSYNC, but in 2002, he became a solo singer. His song 'Cry me a River' was the winner of an important music award. Justin Timberlake wears great clothes, and he's a really cool dancer, too.

**2** Look at the poster on page 100. Are the sentences true or false? Correct the false sentences.

1 Robbie Williams writes songs.
2 Robbie wasn't in a band.
3 Avril Lavigne can't play a musical instrument.
4 Avril was famous when she was sixteen years old.
5 Justin Timberlake's band was *Take That*.
6 Justin received an award for his dancing.

# Vocabulary

**3** Match the words in the box with the pictures.

songwriter   solo singer   album   fans   award

① ② ③ ④ ⑤

**4** Match the definitions with the words from exercise 3.

1 This person sings, but isn't in a band.
2 This is a type of prize.
3 These people like pop stars.
4 A CD or cassette with a lot of songs on it.
5 This person writes songs.

# Speaking

**5** Ask and answer the questions.

Who's your favourite music star?

Where is he/she from?

What does he/she look like?

Does he/she play a musical instrument?

What are some of his/her famous songs?

# Writing

**6** Choose three music stars and write notes.

| name | _____ |
| nationality | _____ |
| how did he/she start? | _____ |
| famous songs/albums | _____ |
| why do you like this person? | _____ |

**7** Write descriptions of your music stars. Find photos or draw pictures to make a poster. Use the project guide to help you.

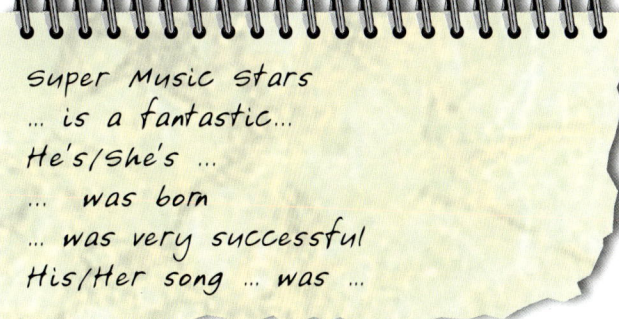

Super Music Stars
... is a fantastic...
He's/She's ...
... was born
... was very successful
His/Her song ... was ...

**8** Display your poster in the classroom.

# Project 6

## Reading

**1** Read about the characters in a new soap opera. Who is your favourite character? Why?

### My new Soap opera – Hollywood Kids

Hollywood Kids is a fantastic soap opera. It's about children at a school in California. Their parents are all millionaires. The children live in big houses and they all wear really fashionable clothes.

These are the main characters.

This is Scott. He's eleven. He loves music because his mum is a rock singer. He can play the electric guitar. He's really popular and he wears fantastic clothes! He usually wears blue jeans and nice jackets. His dad is a film director.

Helen is twelve and she's great. She loves fashion and she wants to be an actress or a model. Her mum is a model and her dad is a photographer. Helen buys new clothes every weekend! She wears expensive skirts and dresses, and she's really pretty.

Enrique is twelve. He's Scott's best friend. He's really good at sport and he plays in the school American football team. He's a fantastic player and he's very good-looking, too! His dad's a famous basketball player and his mum is an actress. Enrique usually wears really expensive trainers.

**2** Look at the poster on page 102 and complete the notes.

1  The children go to school in _____.
2  They live in big _____.
3  Scott's mum is a _____.
4  Enrique wears expensive _____.
5  Helen wants to be an _____.
6  She buys a lot of _____.

# Vocabulary

**3** Find words in the poster and match them with the pictures.

**4** Complete the sentences with the words from exercise 3.

1  I want to work in the theatre because I'm a good _____.
2  Steven Spielberg is a great _____.
3  He's really tall. He's a fantastic _____.
4  My aunt won the lottery and now she's a _____.
5  My dad has got a great camera. He's a _____.
6  My cousin is very pretty. She's a _____.

# Speaking

**5** Look again at the poster. Ask and answer questions about the characters in the soap opera.

> Who is the best looking?

> Who has got the most exciting life?

> Who wears the nicest clothes?

> Who has got the most interesting parents?

> Who would you like to be?

# Writing

**6** Invent your own soap opera. Think of three characters and write notes.

character 1
name          _____
age           _____
parents       _____
interests     _____
clothing      _____

**7** Think of a name for your soap opera and write descriptions of your characters. Add photos or draw pictures to make poster. Use the project guide to help you.

My new soap opera – .......
... is a fantastic soap opera. It's about ...
These are the main characters.
This is ...
He's/She's ...
His/Her mum is ...
He/She usually wears ...

**8** Display your poster in the classroom.

# Young heroes

## Meet the Characters

**Anna**     **Harry**     **Mark**     **Lucy**     **Tim**     **Jason Chain**     **Teacher**

**Chorus**     This is a story with a moral to tell. So make sure that you listen well.

## Scene 1

**Narrator**     Mark and Lucy are in the park.
*(Lucy and Mark enter)*

**Lucy**     It's really hot. What shall we do?

**Mark**     Let's play football.

**Lucy**     I want to go to the lake.

**Mark**     All right. Come on!

## Scene 2

**Narrator**     Mark and Lucy are at the lake. Suddenly, they hear a shout.

**Tim**     Help, Help!

**Mark**     *(Listening)* Who's shouting?

**Tim**     Help! Help!

**Lucy**     Look! There's a boy in the lake.

**Mark**     He's holding on to a piece of wood.

**Tim**     Help me! I can't swim!

**Lucy**     What shall we do?

**Mark**     I don't know. It's dangerous.

**Tim**     *(Waving and shouting)* Help! Please help me!

**Lucy**     I'm scared.

# Scene 3

| | |
|---|---|
| **Narrator** | Anna and Harry arrive. *(Harry and Anna enter)* |
| **Lucy** | Look! Harry and Anna are coming. |
| **Mark** | Harry! Anna! There's a boy in the lake. |
| **Anna** | He can't swim! |
| **Harry** | Let's save him! |
| **Mark** | Good idea. You can help him. We're late. |
| **Lucy** | Bye! *(Mark and Lucy exit)* |
| **Chorus** | Mark and Lucy aren't brave today. So they decide to go away. |

# Scene 4

| | |
|---|---|
| **Narrator** | Anna and Harry rescue the boy. |
| **Tim** | Help me! |
| **Anna** | How can we save him? What can we do? |
| **Harry** | Let's phone the police. |
| **Anna** | No, Harry. There isn't time. We must help him now. |
| **Harry** | Let's find a branch. He can hold on to it. We can pull him out of the water. |
| **Anna** | Good idea! *(Harry and Anna look for a branch)* |
| **Tim** | Help! |
| **Harry** | *(Holding a branch)* Hold this branch. We're going to pull you out! |
| **Tim** | OK. *(Holds on to the branch)* |
| **Anna and Harry** | *(Pulling)* Pull! Pull! It's working! |
| **Chorus** | The children are heroes. So they save Tim Now they can be friends with him. |

# Scene 5

| | |
|---|---|
| **Narrator** | Anna and Harry meet Tim. |
| **Anna** | Are you OK? |
| **Tim** | Yes, thank you. But I'm wet and cold. |
| **Harry** | Here, take my jacket. *(Harry gives his jacket to Tim)* |
| **Tim** | Thank you. You saved my life. |
| **Harry** | I'm Harry. This is Anna. |
| **Tim** | I'm Tim. Let's be friends. |
| **Harry** | Of course! We'll walk home with you. |

# Scene 6

| | |
|---|---|
| **Narrator** | The children walk home with Tim. |
| **Anna** | Where do you live? |
| **Tim** | I live in Manchester. |
| **Harry** | Manchester? But we're in London! |
| **Tim** | Yes. I'm staying in a hotel in London with my dad. He's doing some concerts here. |
| **Harry** | Concerts? |
| **Tim** | Yes. He's a singer. *(stopping)* Here's our hotel. |
| **Anna** | *(surprized)* Wow! It's huge. *(Jason enters)* Look! There's Jason Chain! He's my favourite pop star! |
| **Tim** | Yeah. He's my dad. |
| **Harry** | Your dad? Wow! He's fantastic! |
| **Tim** | Yes, he is. Thanks for saving my life! I'll tell my dad. See you soon! |
| **Anna** | See you. |
| **Tim** | Bye! |
| | *(Anna and Harry exit)* |
| **Chorus** | Anna, Harry and Tim Become good friends Now listen to how our story ends. |

# Scene 7

| | |
|---|---|
| **Narrator** | Monday morning at school. |
| **Teacher** | Good morning, children. |
| **Chorus** | Good morning, Miss! |
| **Teacher** | Yesterday, Harry Barton and Anna Hall did something very brave. They saved a boy's life. And that boy has a very famous dad. Children ... meet our special guest. *(Jason and Tim enter)* |
| **Lucy** | Wow! It's Jason Chain! |
| **Mark** | And there's that boy from the lake! |
| **Jason** | Hi, everybody. Hello Anna and Harry! |
| **Anna and Harry** | Hello Jason. Hi Tim! |
| **Mark** | Hey! That's cool! Anna and Harry know Jason Chain! |
| **Jason** | I want to say 'thank you' to Harry and Anna. They're young heroes. And now I want to sing a few songs for you ... *(begins to play)* |
| **Chorus** | Thank you for coming to our play. We hope you listen to what we say. Think of others every day. |

# Past simple: irregular verbs

| Base form | Past simple |
|---|---|
| be | was/were |
| become | became |
| bring | brought |
| build | built |
| buy | bought |
| catch | caught |
| come | came |
| cost | cost |
| cut | cut |
| do | did |
| eat | ate |
| find | found |
| fly | flew |
| forget | forgot |
| get up | got up |
| give | gave |
| go | went |
| have | had |
| hide | hid |
| leave | left |
| make | made |
| meet | met |
| put | put |
| run | ran |
| see | saw |
| send | sent |
| sing | sang |
| sit | sat |
| steal | stole |
| swim | swam |
| take | took |
| tell | told |
| think | thought |
| throw | threw |
| understand | understood |
| wear | wore |
| win | won |

# OXFORD
UNIVERSITY PRESS

Great Clarendon Street, Oxford OX2 6DP

Oxford University Press is a department of the University of Oxford.
It furthers the University's objective of excellence in research, scholarship,
and education by publishing worldwide in

Oxford New York

Auckland Cape Town Dar es Salaam Hong Kong Karachi
Kuala Lumpur Madrid Melbourne Mexico City Nairobi
New Delhi Shanghai Taipei Toronto

With offices in

Argentina Austria Brazil Chile Czech Republic France Greece
Guatemala Hungary Italy Japan Poland Portugal Singapore
South Korea Switzerland Thailand Turkey Ukraine Vietnam

OXFORD and OXFORD ENGLISH are registered trade marks of
Oxford University Press in the UK and in certain other countries

First published 2007

2016 2015

16 15 14 13 12

**No unauthorized photocopying**

ISBN: 978 0 19 480600 8 Pack
ISBN: 978 0 19 480612 1 Book

Printed in China

This book is printed on paper from certified and well managed sources.

Schválilo MŠMT čj. 27747/2007-22 dne 21.1.2008 k zařazení do seznamu
učebnic pro základní vzdělávání jako součást ucelené řady učebnic pro
vzdělávací obor anglický jazyk s dobou platnosti 6 let.
Recenzentkami jsou Mgr. Zdeňka Křížová a PhDr. Ivana Pekařová.

ACKNOWLEDGEMENTS

*We would like to thank the following for their kind permission to reproduce
photographs*: Action Plus, pp.30 (female gymnast), 32 (Tim Duncan), Alamy
Images, pp.10 (Edinburgh Castle), 12 (h & s boy, girl in New York), 18 (iguana),
29 (girl & tennis racket), 38 (shoe shaped house), p.45 (boy and girl/Gaetano
Images), 46 (h & s boy), 47 (boy at Notting Hill Carnival), 55 (2 schools girls),
77 (schoolkids/Janine Wiedel Photolibrary), 88 (Sun City pool, lions on
Safari), 102 (boy with guitar/Chris Warren) Aquarius Library, pp.24 (Fred
Flintstone & Barney Rubble), 74 (James Bond's car chase) Bubbles
Photolibrary, p.68 (h & s teenage boy), Corbis, pp.12 (Oxford rooftops), 13
(China town, New York), 21 (schoolchildren/Randy Faris),26 (h & s girl), 38
(Futuro house, elephant shaped house), 40 (h & s girl, Coober Pedy
underground house, Bedouin boy, Bedouin tent), 44 (La Tomatina), 52 (aerial
view Australian outback, Australian cowboys & cattle), 54 (h & s teenage boy),
58 (3 children on slide, rollercoaster ride), 59 (boy on mobile phone), 60 (h & s
smiling girl), 71 (h & s boy), 72 (baby Orang Utan, h & s girl), 74 (h & s boy), 75
(4 teenage friends), 92 (Liverpool/Richard Klune), 100 (Robbie
Williams/Stephane Cardinale/People Avenue, Justin Timberlake/Reuters),
102 (boy with football/Richard Hamilton Smith) Corel, p.60 (Houses of
Parliament), Digital Vision, p.72 (jungle leaf), Education Photos, pp 32 (h & s
boy), 54 (h & s schoolgirl), 74 (schoolchildren in uniform), Empics/P.A., p.66
(Dino, Junior Eurovision 2004, Sakis Rouvas, Eurovision 2004), Getty Images,
pp.7 (dancers), 9 (girl in uniform), 10 (2 girls together, h & s girl), 12 (Japanese
boy), 18 (school classroom), 26 (h & s boy), 30 (boy & football), 41 (boy's untidy
room), 44 (Venice Carnival, children carrying Chinese lanterns), 46 (Rio
Carnival parade), 54 (schoolgirl at desk), 60 (news reporter), 68 (h & s teenage
girl), 82 (girl shopping for shoes), 92 (two girls in tree/Tara Moore) Idols
Licensing & Publicity Ltd pp.92 (Eminem/Jonathan Mannion), 100 (Avril
Lavigne/Dalle), Jacqui Hurst Photography, p.80 (detail of denim jeans, detail
of woollen scarf), John Foxx, p.102 (young girl), Kobal Collection Ltd, p.24 (the
Flintstones & the Rubbles), Photodisc, pp.9 (schoolboy), 67 (girl playing guitar),
Popperfoto, p.29 (Roberto Carlos), 33 (Capt Zagorakis & team Euro 2004), Pow-
erStock/Superstock Ltd, pp.18 (h & s boy), 26 (extended family), 46 (h & s girl),
59 (girl on mobile phone), 71 (h & s girl), Punchstock p.92 (kids in
tent/Photodisc), Redferns Music Picture Library, pp.10 (Evanescence); 68
(Beyonce), 69 (Britney Spears), Rex Features Ltd, pp 15 (young girl & rabbit),
52 (School of the Air student), 80 (chocolate fashion, Matthew McGrory &
largest shoe), Zefa Visual Media UK Ltd p.35 (two girls/Kevin Dodge).

*Illustrations by*: Kathy Baxendale, pp.15 (pets), 21 (grammar ex 8), 25 (grammar
ex 6), 43 (food), 45 (food), 79 (clothes shop), 81 (clothes), 87 (the weather),
92 (project 1), 94 (project 2), 96 (project 3), 98 (project 4), 100 (project 5),
102 (project 6), Mark Draisey, pp.7 (teacher in classroom), 15 (schoolboy
friends), 31 (boys at computer), 35 (grammar ex 8), 37 (girl & mum), 49 (school
cafeteria), 55 (girl waiting for friends), 61 (boy writing), 67 (boy playing
guitar), 76 (musical instruments), 87 (robot teacher, astronauts), 91 (teenage
friends), 101, 104, 105, 106 Mark Duffin, pp.6, 7 (classroom), 16 (teenage
children), 21 (girls looking at photos), 32 (quiz show), 37 (boy's untidy
bedroom), 45 (supermarket trolley), 53 (school of the air student), 72 (tv
review), 73 (tv programmes), 82 (children wearing horrible clothes),
86, 88 (quiz competition), Richard Duszczak, pp.20 (American girl), 27 (family
at home), 34 (family tree), 43 (kitchen), 48 (boy's bedroom), 51 (students in
classroom), 77 (grammar ex 6), 81 (3 teenage girls), 85 (holidays), Martina
Farrow, pp.5, 16 (reading ex 4), 17 (possessions), 31 (sports), 37 (bedroom
objects), 44 (reading ex 4), 48 (things for a party), 53 (school subjects),
67 (musical instruments), 79 (accessories), 83 (writing ex 7), 93, 97, Andre
Labrie, pp.11 (grammar ex 6), 17 (grammar), 20 (pets), 25 (family tree),
34 (sports), 39 (grammar ex 7), 43 (fridge interior), 49, (grammar ex 7),
51 (grammar ex 5), 57 (children in museum), 59 (places in town), 62 (places in
a town), 73 (grammar ex 6), 76 (vocabulary ex 4), 90 (the weather), 99, Chris
Pavely, pp.9 (grammar ex 3), 23 (grammar ex 4), 37 (grammar ex 3),
51 (grammar ex 4), 57 (grammar ex 3), 71 (grammar ex 3), 79 (grammar ex 3),
85 (grammar ex 3), Andy Peters, pp.9 (schoolboys), 19 (girl with pet), 20 (possessions), 21 (boy's bedroom), 48 (food shopping), 57 (places to visit), 62 (places to visit), 63 (grammar ex 8), 65 (grammar ex 3), 77 (kids' party), 85 (teenage
friends), 89 (writing ex 6, ex 7), 90 (clothes), 95, 103, Martin
Shovel, pp.4 (schoolboy), 11 (grammar ex 8), 17 (grammar ex 6), 19 (boy
writing), 27 (writing ex 8), 35 (football game), 59 (girl & diary), 63 (basketball
game), 65 (schoolboys in playground), 71 (adjectives), 83 (writing ex 7),
91 (grammar ex 7 & 8).

*Cover Illustration by*: Chris Pavely

*Main Story Illustration by*: Chris Pavely

*Song Illustrations by*: Martina Farrow

*Picture Research & Artwork Commissioning by*: Mandy Twells

*Songs by*: Jenny Quintana